Dictionary of Music Terms and Chords

BY ALBERT DeVITO, PH. D., MUS. D.

KENYON PUBLICATIONS

EXCLUSIVELY DISTRIBUTED BY

HAL•LEONARD® CORPORATION

7777 W. BLUEMOUND RD. P.O. BOX 13819 MILWAUKEE, WI 53213

DICTIONARY *of* MUSIC TERMS *and* CHORDS
(Updated Version)

By
Albert DeVito, *Ph.D., Mus.D.*

Copyright © 1995
KENYON PUBLICATIONS

ISBN 0-934286-69-8 (Soft Cover)

Library of Congress
Catalogue Card Number
95-79742
Library of Congress
Cataloging-in-Publication Data

Distribution by
Hal Leonard Corporation
7777 W. Bluemound Road
P.O. Box 13819
Milwaukee, WI 53213 (USA)
        414/774-3630: Phone
        414/774-3259: FAX
        26668: Telex

Made and Printed in U.S.A.

PREFACE

Music Terminology has taken a vast leap forward within the past ten years from its past heritage heading for the twenty-First Century. Traditional terms are still a strong force, especially from the Italian, French and German languages. However since then, new technology has taken over which has wedged its way through since the beginning of MIDI *(Musical Instruments Digital Interface).*

Perhaps to the traditional musician, these terms may appear strange. The door has opened with new possibilities unforeseen. We have now enter the Fifth Generation of Computer Technology since the vacuum tube.

> *First Generation* - vacuum tubes
> *Second Generation* - transistors
> *Third Generation* - intergrated circuits
> *Fourth Generation* - new and smaller circuits
> *Fifth Generation* - easier technology capable of
>   understanding the human voice.

In relationship to CD-ROM, the wealth of knowledge is unbelievable. Beyond all of this, future generations will have new UNIVERSES of exploration for research and will add to this as new frontiers step into the picture.

It is the author's wish that this dictionary will be a new beginning for those with a traditional background for further exploration.

There will be no limit as to where this will all lead as the UNIVERSE is limitless and timeless. Mankind can only limit him/her self until the unseen ties are broken. When this happens, we can all realize that we are all ONE, Always have been and Always will be. Progress will be continued without any barriers of negativity which put halters on a wonderment of activity.

Blessed be with UNIVERSAL LOVE I am

> *Albert DeVito*

DICTIONARY OF MUSIC TERMS AND CHORDS
(Updated Version)

CONTENTS

ABBREVIATIONS

(ACRONYMS ARE INCLUDED IN THE MAIN TEXT.)

An Acronym is a letter formed from the first, or first few letters of a series of words. An example of this would be *LCD* in which the full name is *Liquid Crystal Display*. This shows the letters, numbers, instruments and other information that are being used on a synthesizer, digital piano or organ. It is the friend of the performer as it displays what is being used or any changes made.

accel.	accelerando
accomp.	accompaniment
Adg° *or* **ad°**	Adagio
ad lib. *or* **ad libit.**	ad libitum
A e v i a.	Alleluia
affett°	affettuoso
affrett°	affrettando
ag° *or* **agit,**	agitato
All°.	Allegro
Allgett°.	Allegretto
all' ott.	all' ottava
al seg.	al segno
Andto.	Andantino
Andte	Andante
Anim°	Animato
arc.	arcato, or coll' arco
arp°.	arpeggio
a t. *or* **a tem.**	a tempo
B.C. *or* **Bass Con.**	basso continuo
Bl.	Bläser
Br.	Bratschen
Brill.	brillante
c. a.	coll' arco
cad.	cadenza
C.B.	Contra-bass
cal.	calando
calm.	calmato
cant.	canto
cantab.	cantabile
c.d.	colla destra
c.f.	canto fermo
'cello.	violoncello
cemb.	cembalo

Ch.	choir organ
Clar.	clarinet
Clar°.	clarino
col c.	col canto
coll' ott.	coll' ottava
c. 8va.	coll' ottava
con espr.	con espressione
cont.	contano
Cor.	corno
c.p.	colla parte
cres.	crescendo
c. s.	colla sinistra
c s. *or* **co. so.**	come sopra
Cto	concerto
c.v o c.	cola voce
d.	destra, droite
D.C.	da capo
D.C.S.R.	da capo senza replica, *or* senza ripetizione
Dec.	decani
decres.	decrescendo
dest.	destra
Diap.	diapasons
dim.	diminuendo
div.	divisi
dol.	dolce
dolciss.	dolcissimo
dopp. ped.	doppio pedale ˎ
D.S.	dal segno
esp. *or* **espres.**	espressivo
Eng.	English
f.	forte
Fag.	fagotto
ff.	fortissimo

fff.	fortississimo	Org.	organ
Fl.	flauto	Ott., Ova, *or* 8va.	ottava
F.O.	full organ	*p.*	piano
fp.	forte piano	p. a. p.	poco a poco
fz. *or* forz.	forzato	Ped.	pedal
Fr.	French	Perd.	Perdendosi
G.	gauche	P. F.	Più forte
Ger.	German	Piang.	Piangendo
G.O.	great organ	Pianiss.	Pianissimo
Gr.	Greek	Pizz.	Pizzicato
Graz°.	grazioso	*pp*	Pianissimo
Haut.	hautboy	*ppp.*	Pianississimo
Hizbl.	Holzbläser	Rall.	Rallentando
Hr. *or* Hrn.	Hörner	Rf., rfz., *or* rinf.	Rinforzando
Intro.	Introduction	R . H. .	Right Hand
It.	Italian	Ritar.	Ritardando
K.F.	Kleine Flöte	Riten., *or* Rit.	Ritenuto
L.	Left	S	Senza
Lat.	Latin	Seg.	Segue
leg.	legato, leger	Sfz.	Sforzando
legg.	leggiero	Sinf.	Sinfonia
l.h.	left hand/link hand	Smorz.	Smorzando
lusing.	lusingando	Sp., Spa.	Spanish
M.	manual	S. S., *or* S. sord.	Senza sord
Magg.	Maggiore	Sos.	Sostenuto
manc.	mancando	Stacc.	Staccato
marc.	marcato	String.	Stringendo
m.d.	mano destra	Sym.	Symphony
	or, main droite	Tem.	Tempo
men.	meno	Tem. 1°	Tempo prim
mez.	mezzo	Ten.	Tenuto
mf	mezzo forte	Timb.	timballes
m.g.	main gauche	Timp.	timpani
M.M.	Maelzel's	T.S.	tasto solo
	Metronome	Tr.	Trill
mod. *or* modto.	moderato	Trem.	Tremolando
mor.	morendo	U.	Una
mp	mezzo piano	U.C.	Una corda
MS.	manuscript	Unis.	Unison
m. s.	mano sinistra	V.	Voce, Volti
Mus.Bac.	Bachelor of Music	Va.	Viola
Mus.B.	Bachelor of Music	Vc. *or* Vcllo.	violoncello
Mus.D.	Doctor of Music	viv.	vivace
m. v.	mezza voce	Vno., *or* Viol.	Violin
Ob.	oboe	VS.	Volti subito
Obb.	obbligato	Vv.	violini

A

A The sixth tone of the diatonic major scale of C. In the A minor scale (relative minor of C) it is the first note. It is the first tone in the diatonic major scale of A.

A *(It.)* By; for; to; at; in.

A ballata: *(It.)* In the style of a simple dance (see *ballata*).

Abandon *(Fr.)* With ease.

A battuta *(It.)* In strict time.

Abbandonasi, Abbandono *(It.)* Without restraint: with passionate expression.

Académie de Musique *(Fr.)* An academy of music with professors and students, also a society for promoting musical culture.

Académie spirituelle *(Fr.)* A concert of sacred music.

Accarezzévola *(It.)* In a persuasive and caressing manner.

Accarezzevolménte *(It.)* Caressing, coaxing.

A cappella *(It.)* Vocal music without accompaniment.

A cappriccio *(It.)* In a capricious style; in a free style according to the taste of the performer.

Accelerándo *(It.)* (abb. Accel.) Gradually increasing the rate of speed or tempo.

Acceleráto *(It.)* Accelerated rapidity.

Accent *(Fr.)*, **Accénto, Accénti** *(It.)* A stress or emphasis upon a specific tone, chord or beat.

Accessory notes. Those notes one degree above and one degree below the principal note of a turn.

Acciaccatura *(It.)* A very short grace note (♪) an accessory placed before the principal note with the accent on the principal note.

Accidentals Sharps, flats or naturals placed before notes to raise or lower a tone that are not found in the Key Signature.

Sharp, Double Sharp, Flat, Double Flat, Natural

♯   𝄪   ♭   ♭♭   ♮

Accompaniment. An added part or parts to support a solo voice(s) or instrument.

Accopiáto *(It)* Tied or joined together.

Accord *(Fr.)* **Accordo** *(It.)* A chord, consonance, concord.

Accordándo *(It.)* Refers to tuning.

Accordion *(Fr.)* A keyboard instrument with bellows, containing bass buttons that sound chords or single notes when played.

Accrescéndo *(It.)* Increase in tone and power.

Achromatic music A simple type of music where few accidentals are used.

Acht *(Ger.)* Eight.

Acoust Used for **A**coustic or **A**coustics on a MIDI instrument as it takes less space on the **LCD**.

Acoustics The science of sound.

Action The workings or mechanism of a piano or organ.

Active Sensing is a MIDI message indicating that the MIDI line is working.

A/D An analog signal changed to a digital signal.

Adagietto *(It.)* Little faster than Adagio.

Adagio *(It.)* Slowly.

Adagio assai *(It.)* Very slow *(di molto).*

ADC Refers to Analog to Digital Converter. This device converts an analog sound to a digital signal.

Addolorato *(It.)* Sorrowful.

A demi jeu *(Fr.)* Half power of instrument.

A deux *(Fr.)* For two instruments or voices.

A deux mains *(Fr.)* For two hands.

Adjunct notes Unaccented auxiliary notes.

Ad libitum *(Lat.)* (abb., **Ad lib.**) At will, pleasure or omit.

Adornaménte *(It.)* Gaily, neatly, elegantly.

Adornaménto *(It.)* An ornament or embellishment.

ADSR is an acronym or abbreviation for Attack, Decay, Sustain and Release which would be the four stages of an **A**DSR envelope in production of a sound.

A due, or **A2** *(It.)* A duet. For two voices or instruments.

Adulatoriamente *(It.)* A caressing flattering manner.

A duo corde *(It.)* Upon two strings.

A dur *(Ger.)* The key of A major.

Advanced Frequency Modulation (AFM) provides a superior advance in FM sound, quality and programming versatility.

Advanced Wave Memory relates to *Advanced Frequency Modulation,* see *AWM* and *AWM2.*

AES refers to the *Audio Engineering Society.* It is a professional association of sound engineers with their headquarters located in New York, NY. Chapters are located throughout the world.

Affable *(It.)* In a pleasing agreeable manner.

Affannato *(It.)* Sad and distressed.

Affannoso *(It.)* With anxious expression.

Affectirt *(Ger.)* **Affectueux** *(Fr.)* **Affettatament** *(It.)* Affectionate.

AFM refers to **A**udio Frequency Modulation. It provides a superior advance in FM sound, quality and programming versatility. It is also an abbreviation for **A**merican **F**ederation of **M**usicians. (see *Advanced Frequency Modulation).*

AFM2 is a second generation of *Advanced Frequency Modulation.*

Aftertouch is pressure sensitivity on a key (keys of a piano, organ or keyboard) which allows **M**IDI controller information to be sent after key is struck (see *Touch Tone).*

Aftertouch/Pressure is the amount of pressure applied to keys after being depressed.

Affettuoso *(It.)* with tenderness and passionate expression.

Affrettando, Affrettate, Affrettoso *(It.)* Hurrying the time.

Agilita *(It.)* Lightness.

Agilménte *(It.)* Lively and gay.

Agitamento, Agitato *(It.)* Agitated, hurried, restless.

Agitato *(It.)* Agitated, restless, hurried.

Agnus Dei *(Lat.)* Lamb of God. A movement in a Mass.

Ai *(It.)* To the; in the style of.

Air A short song, melody or tune, with or without words.

Ais *(Ger.)* The note 'A' Sharp.

Alberti Bass *(It.)* Broken chords used in the bass.

Al fine *(It.)* To the end.

Al fine, e poi la coda *(It.)* After playing to the *Fine* measure, go on to the coda.

Al, All', Alla, Alle, Agli, Allo *(It.)* To the; in the style or manner of.

Algorithm refers to a decision or choice that has to be made. If one has a 8-voice polyphonic instrument, what happens if a person plays nine or ten notes? What notes are turned off? Much depends on the make of the instrument. The outer sounds may be held; the first note could be dropped, or the softest. One should experiment with their instrument to see what the possibilities are. This would be called Channel-Stealing-Algorithm.

Algorithmic Composition is when the computer makes music decisions based upon parameters defined by the user. Effects can be brought out as reverb, chorus, delay, the size of a room, stage, hall or auditorium, effects as to brightness, normal or warm.

Aliasing is simply noise that can occur during an analog-to-digital conversion process. This could be caused by oversampling anti-aliasing filters that block signals above a particular frequency.

Alla breve *(It.)* $\frac{2}{2}$ Time, sometimes called *cut-time* ¢ .

Alla caccia *(It.)* Hunting style.

Alla camera *(It.)* Chamber music style.

Alla marcia *(It.)* March style.

Allargando *(It.)* Growing broader, louder and slower.

Allegraménte *(It.)***Allegrement** (Fr.) Gaily, joyfully, quickly.

Allegretto *(It.)* Slower than Allegro, light and cheerful.

Allegríssimo: *(It.)* Extremely quick and lively.

Allégro *(It. and Fr.)* Quick and lively.

Allégro agitato *(It.)* Quick with anxiety and agitation.

Allégro appassionato *(It.)* Passionately quick.

Allégro assi *(It.)* very quick.

Allégro con brio *(It.)* Quick with brilliancy.

Allégro con fuoco: *(It.)* Quick with animation and fire.

Allégro con moto *(It.)* Quick with more movement.

Allégro giusto *(It.)* Quick with exactness

Allégro ma non troppo *(It.)* Quick but not too fast.

Allégro moderato *(It.)* Moderately fast.

Allégro molto *(It.)* Fast and animated.

Allégro vivace *(It.)* Very rapid with vivacity.

Alléluia *(Fr.)* **Allelujah** *(Heb.)* is an expression of praise as *Hallelujah, Praise the Lord.*

Allemande *(Fr.)* The first dance movement in an old suite.

All Notes Off A MIDI message that turns off any notes sounding when not wanted. A **P**anic **B**utton will achieve the same effect.

Al loco *(It.)* To the previous place.

All' ottava *(It.)* A direction to play the octave higher or lower. It is sometimes directed as *8va* or *All' 8va.*

Al piacere *(It.)* At pleasure.

Al Segno *(It.)* (abb. Al Seg.) Return to the sign.

Alto *(It.)* Generally applied to the lowest female voice.

Alto clef The C clef used on the third line of the staff.

Amabile *(It.)* Gently, graceful.

A mezza voce *(It.)* In a subdued tone.

A moll *(Ger.)* Key of A minor.

Amore *(It.)* Tenderness, love and affection.

Amplifier is commonly known as a loudspeaker. It supplies power and strengthens an incoming signal for output. It could be an analog voltage-controlled amplifier, VCA. The VDA is a variable digital amplifier. The VCA and VDA determines the loudness of the synthesized sound.

Amplitude refers to the size of a measured signal from "0 dB" *(sound of the human voice)* level to a higher peak *(pain starts at 140 dB).* This can apply to an electrical, an acoustical signal, a sound, or any other signal that is shaped like a wave. It can be the loudness of a sound or the brightness of a light.

An *(Ger.)* On; to; Organ music, draw or add.

Anacrusis refers to one or more unaccented syllables or notes at the beginning of a line of verse or music followed by an accented syllable or note. In music it is commonly referred to as an *Upbeat.*

Analog (Analogue) A process with an output that is continuous like a voltage wave form. Tracks are laid down to tape in a linear sequence. It is a continuous variable signal as a soundwave form. This is used fortape recording. It is in contrast with Digital data (see *Digital).*

Ancora *(It.)* Repeat.

Andamento *(It.)* Rather slow in style of *Andante.*

Andante *(It.)* In moderate time, flowing easily and gracefully. It may be modified by the addition of other words.

Andante affettuoso *(It.)* Slow with tender feelings.

Andante cantabile *(It.)* Slowly in a singing style.

Andante con moto *(It.)* Moving easily with motion.

Andante grazioso *(It.)* Moderately slow and graceful.

Andante maestoso *(It.)* Slowly in a majestic style.

Andante ma non troppo *(It.)* Not too slow.

Andante pastorale *(It.)* Moderately slow pastoral style.

Andante sostenuto *(It.)* Slowly and sustained.

Andantino *(It.)* Means a little slower than Andante. Now it is generally used as meaning faster. It is an ambiguous word in reality, bearing much disagreement.

Anima *(It.)* Soul, spirit, animation.

Animáto *(It.)* Animated with life and spirit.

Animosissimo *(It.)* Bold and resolute.

Anmuthig *(Ger.)* Agreeable and sweet.

Antecedent The first phrase of a musical period; the subject of a fugue or canon.

Antialiasing Technique for smoothing audio or visual data.

A passo a passo *(It.)* Step by step.

A piacere, A piacimento *(It.)* At the pleasure of the performer.

A poco a poco *(It.)* By little and little.

A poco piu lento *(It.)* A little slower.

A poco piu mosso *(It.)* A little faster.

Appassionato *(It.)* Passionately, with much emotion and feeling.

Apple Desktop Bus The built in circuitry of Apple Computers for input devices as keyboards, mice, trackballs. These are mounted on the back panel labeled with icons.

Applications are software programs one uses to create input as with a Word Processor, Spreadsheet, Database, Graphics, Music, and more.

Application Template A ready made file to help the user create designs or documents (see *Style Sheet, Template*). This could be in the form of manuscript paper which is music writing paper, consisting of five lines and four spaces.

Appoggiatura *(It.)* A note of embellishment.

A punta d'arco *(It.)* With the point of the bow.

A quatre mains *(Fr.)* **A quattro mani** *(It.)* For four hands.

Arabesque or **Arabesk** An ornament or embellished work.

Arc. Abb. of **Arco**, meaning *bow.*

Arcáto *(It.)* played with a bow.

Ardente *(It.)* With fire.

Ardito *(It.)* Bold with energy.

Ardore *(It.)* With ardor and warmth.

Aria *(It.)* An air; a tune; a song sung by one voice, either with or without an accompaniment.

Armonioso *(It.)* Harmonious.

Arpa *(It. or Spa.)* The harp.

Arpegger *(Fr.)* **Arpegglamento, Arpeggiándo, Arpeggiáto** *(It.)* Music played arpeggio fashioned in the style of a harp which is indicated by a wavy line in piano music. ( )

Arpéggio *(It.)* Playing in a harp like manner. In piano or organ music, it is indicated by a wavy line before two or more notes. Notes of a chord played quickly, one after the other *(see **A**rpegger).*

Arpeggio Chord An harmonic background accompaniment. It may be synchronized with rhythm based upon notes, keys, sounded when played on either electronic, digital or Midi keyboard. This depends on what the manufacturer, or user has programmed.

Arrangement (abb., **Arr.** or **Arrang.**) A selection or adaptation of a composition, or parts of it to instrument(s) for which it was not originally written or designed. Sometimes referred to as a *Chart.*

Arsis *(Gr.)* Light accent of measure. An up-beat. Last beat of a measure.

As *(Ger.)* "A" flat.

As dur *(Ger.)* Key of "A" flat major.

Assai *(It.)* Very, extremely.

Assez *(Fr.)* Enough, sufficient.

Assez lent *(Fr.)* Quite slow.

A suo comodo *(It.)* Synonymous with ad libitum.

Asychronous Transmission is controlled by start and stop bits at the beginning and end of each character. These are not controlled by a clock signal. Signals from a keyboard, piano and computer are *Asychronous* because the keys are pressed at irregular intervals. Signals from a disk are close synchronous signals, where the time between the signals are always the same.

A tempo (*abb.* **A tem., A temp.**) *(It.)* In time after some relaxatio or deviation of the time, the performer(s) return to the original movement.

A to D Refers to a change from *Analog* coding signals to *Digital* coding signals (see *A/D, Analog and Digital).*

ATR *Audio Tape Recorder.*

Attacca *(It.)* Go on. Begin the next.

Attack The start of a musical note *(see Envelope)* or the first part of a sound which is defined as to the amount of time it takes for the sound or signal to rise from silence to the loudest degree of sound.

Attenuation A process of decreasing the amplitude of a signal (sound) as it moves from one particle of sound to another.

Atto di cadenza *(It.)* A cadence may be introduced.

Audace *(It.)* Bold and spirited.

Audible A sound, capable of being heard.

Audio Sounds that are heard as *music, dialogue* or *narration* within a presentation.

Audio Cassette For recording sound(s) (see *Cassette).*

Audio Dub The recording of a new audio on a tape after the video or movie has been shot *(photographed by camera).* The dubbed audio records directly over one track of the original audio.

Audio Jack A connector on the back panel marked with a sound icon. One can use this audio jack to attach headphones or other audio devices.

Audio Mixing Creating a custom audio track from several different sources using a Mic mixer or other sound mixing devices.

Audio Output A computer output which may be generated by a synthesizer which may resemble musical instruments or a human voice.

Audio Range A frequency that ranges about 15 Hz to 20 kHz which is the common range of audible sound frequencies.

Audiospace The way sound is manipulated to produce a certain audience impression.

Audio Track The part of a video tape that carries the audio signal.

Audio Visual Refers to non-print items as films, tapes, cassettes that record information by sound.

Augmented Intervals that are more than a major or perfect.

Aulodia *(It.)* Singing accompanied by a flute

A una corda *(lt.)* One string. Using the soft pedal in piano playing.
Authentic cadence A cadence in which the chord of the tonic is
preceded by the chord of the dominant (V - I). As an example in
the KEY of "C" the V or dominant chord is "G" which goes to I which is
a "C" Chord.
Automatic Accompaniment Pertains to a program, or a setting
where the accompaniment flows by itself while the user
(performer) plays the melody and chord structure. It may
include several modes for accessing bass patterns, when
playing the accompaniment with one hand, or one finger.
Auto Rhythm Automatically produces various rhythms made from
authentic percussion sounds.
Auxiliary notes Notes that are the next degree above or below an
essential note.
AWM/AWM2 Advanced Wave Memory which is Yamaha's sample
playback format. It uses a 12-bit sample while the AWM2 uses 16-bit.

B

B The seventh tone in the scale of C. It is the first note in the scale of
B having five sharps. In Germany, the note B flat is called B, and B
natural is called H. It is called 'Si' in France and Italy.
Bachelor of Music usually is the first music degree taken at a
university.
Badinage *(Fr.)* Playfulness.
Bagatelle *(Fr.)* A trifle; a toy; a short easy piece of music.
Baldamente *(lt.)* Boldly.
Ballad A simple song, usually in a descriptive form.
Ballade *(Ger.)* Ballata *(lt.)* A dance, also a ballad.
Bank *Storage locations found* in computers, floppy or hard disks,
drum machines, sequencers, synthesizers and/or sound
modules (see *General MIDI*).
Band-reject filter A device that passes on all signals except those
that fall into a specific frequency range. This allows one to stay within
the range of a specified musical instrument.
Bar Perpendicular lines that cross the staff to divide it into measures.
Barcarolle *(Fr.)* A song usually in 6/8 time sung by boatmen in
Venice.
Bar, double Heavy lines drawn vertically across the staff to divide
different parts of a composition, or to show the ending of a piece. Dots
placed at either side of a double-bar mean that either the preceding or
following measures are to be repeated.

Bariton *(Fr.)* **Baritone** *(It.)* **Baritone**   A male voice between the tenor and bass range.

Bass would refer to the lowest voice in a Choral and Orchestral sound. It could refer to a Bass Viol, String Bass and Bass Guitar. Lowest or deepest male voice.

Bassa *(It.)* Low. 8va bassa means to play the notes one octave lower.

Bass clef   The F clef on the fourth line.

Básso continuo *(It.)* is a continued bass line that came into use towards the end of the sixteenth century. It was notated by numbers and used as a guide for playing as chord symbols are used in our day.

Bassoon, Fagott *(Ger.)*, **Faggotto** *(It.)* A double reed wind instrument belonging to the oboe family. It usually forms the bass or deepest tone among the woodwinds.

Básso ostinato *(It.)* A single bass figure constantly repeated.

Bass Parametric Pedal enables a bass guitarist to accommodate any style or type of music.

Bass voice   The lowest male voice.

Baton *(Fr.)* A conductor's stick.

Battere *(It.)* The down stroke in beating time.

Battuta *(It.)* Beat, measure (*A Battuta;* in strict time).

B dur *(Ger.)* B flat major.

Beat   Marking divisions of time by the rise and fall of the hand or baton. A throbbing sound which is heard when two tones are slightly out of unison. An embellishment consisting of the principal note and the note below it making a short trill.

Becken *(Ger.)* Cymbals.

Bed The instrumental component of a jingle.

Bel Canto *(It.)* Applies to singing in a tender, pure and a tender legato style.

Bell   The circular opening at the end of a brass or woodwind instrument.

Bellezza *(It.)* Beauty of tone and expression.

Bellicosamente *(It.)*, **Bellicóso** *(It.)* In a martial and warlike style.

Ben *(It.)* Bene *(It.)* Well, good.

Benedictus *(Lat.)* A part in a Mass.

Ben marcato *(It.)* Well marked with accents.

Berceuse *(Fr.)* A lullaby or cradle song.

Bes *(Ger.)* B double flat; also called Doppel B.

Bidirectional Microphones are sensitive on the front and back but not as sensitive on the sides.

Binary   A form of two divisions, periods or sections.

Bind   A tie, designated by a curved line on the same degree of the staff.

Bit   A single binary digit. It is expressed as "0" or "1" in a digital system.

Bizzaro *(It.)* Whimsical, odd, fantastic.

Bläser *(Ger.)* is an instrument for blowing.

B moll *(Ger.)* Key of B flat minor.

Bolero *(Spa.)* Lively Spanish Dance in $3/4$ time.

Bomb or **bug** reflects an error in the computer or program. A message box is displayed containing a bomb icon to let one know a problem has occurred in the software system. It may cause a *crash*, thus loosing input data. Restart the computer (see *Boot, Crash*).

Boot is the process of starting a computer or other digital instrument. The initial instructions are loaded.

BOT is an acronym for *Beginning Of Tape* which is a mark that shows were to start on a magnetic tape.

Bounce, Bouncing refers to recording several tracks and mixing them. This is then reduced to one or two unused tracks. It is going from one track to another.

Bourree *(Fr.)* An old French dance that is rapid and hearty

Bow An instrument of elastic wood and horsehair, used to set the strings in motion of a violin or a similar instrument. The hair on the bow must have rosin on to cause friction on the strings.

BPM An abbreviation of *Beats per minute* which is a standard method of indicating musical tempo.

Brace A character, either curved or straight, used to connect two or more staves together.

Bratschen *(Ger.)* Violas.

Bravura *(It.)* Bravery, spirit, brilliant, skillful execution.

Breath Controller may be attached to a **MIDI** keyboard. As one plays they may simulate the sounds of breath as if playing a wind instrument.

Bridged mono A method of combining both channels of a certain stero power amplifiers to create a doubly powerful single-channel monaural amplifier.

Brillante *(It.),* **Brillant** *(Fr.)* brillant, bright and sparkling.

Buffer in computer use it is a place where data can be stored temporarily.

Brillante *(It. and Fr.)* Bright, sparkling and brilliant.

Brio *(It.)* Vigor, animation, spirit.

Broken Chords See Arpeggio.

Buffa, Buffo *(It.)* Comic, humorous.

Bug An error that may crash a program (see *Bomb, Crash*).

Buon *(It.)* Good.

Buona nota *(It.)* Accented note.

Buon gusto *(It.)* Good taste. Refinement of style.

Burlando *(It.)* In a playful manner.

Burletta *(It.)* A comic operetta.

Byte A group of 8 bits. A unit of measurement used to rate storage of capacity of disks; one thousand bytes is a kilobyte; one million bytes is a megabyte. A nibble is half a bite.

C

C The first note of the diatonic major scale of **C**. **C** is called *"Ut"* in France and *"Do"* in Italy. **C** also indicates ($\mathbf{C}$) time. When bisected by a vertical line ($\mathbf{\phi}$), Alla Breve or ($\frac{2}{2}$) time is indicated.

Caccia, alla *(It.)* In a hunting style.

Cachucha *(Spa.)* Spanish dance in triple time. It is similar to the Bolero.

Cadence *(Fr.)* A shake or trill, The close of a phrase, either in melody or harmony. The four principal forms of the Cadence in harmony are the whole or authentic; the half; the interrupted and the plagal. The authentic has the dominant chord (V) followed by the tonic (I). The half is the tonic followed by the dominant. The interrupted (deceptive) cadence occurs when the chord of the dominant is followed by any chord except that of the tonic. The plagal cadence has the tonic harmony preceded by the subdominant (IV) chord.

Cadenza *(It.)* An ornamental passage that is introduced near the end of the first and last movement of a composition. It is generally of an impromptu nature.

CAI refers to *Computer Aided Instruction* when a person interacts with a computer in a learning process. In reference to music, these could be progressive lessons in theory, harmony, counterpoint, ear training, instrumental technique, and composition, and more.

Calando *(It.)* Softer and slower by degrees.

Calcando *(It.)* Hurrying the time.

Calma, Calmate, Calmato *(It.)* Calmness, tranquility.

Calore, Caloroso *(It.)* Warmth, passion.

Campana *(It.)* A bell.

Canon A form of contrapuntal composition where each voice or part imitates exactly the melody sung or played by the first voice.

Cantabile *(It.)* In a singing, melodious style with much expression.

Cantando *(It.)* Cantabile.

Cantata *(It.)* **Cantata** *(Fr. and Ger.)* A vocal composition of several movements consisting of airs and recitatives.

Canticle, Cantico *(It.)* **Canticum** *(Lat.)* A non-metrical sacred hymn or song.

Canto *(It.)* A chant or melody, the highest vocal part in choral music.

Cánto clef The C clef, Soprano clef or Treble clef when placed on the first line (see *Clef).*

Cánto fermo *(It.)* A chant or melody.

Cantór *(It. and Lat.)* A singer or chanter.

Cantus firmus *(Lat.)* The plain song or chant. In counterpoint it is the given melody to which the other parts are set.

Capo *(It.)* The head or beginning

Cappélla *(It.)* A chapel, church. Those that play or sing in a church.

Cappélla alla *(It.)* in church style. Vocal chorus without accompaniments. Also known as *A Cappella.*

Cappélla musica *(It.)* church or chapel music.

Capriccio *(It.)* Caprice *(Fr.)* Capriccioso *(It.)* A composition written in a free style.

Cardioid Microphone is a heart shaped microphone. It accepts more sound from ahead, little from the sides and very little from the back.

Caressant *(Fr.)* **Carezzando** *(It.)* **Carezzovole** *(It.)* In a caressing and tender manner.

Caricato *(It.)* **Caricatura** *(It.)* Caricature, exaggerated.

Carillon *(Fr.)* Chime.

Carillons *(Fr.)* Chimes. Bells played by mechanical means or by keyboard. An organ stop.

Carita con *(It.)* With tenderness.

Carol A song of joy, praise and devotion usually sung at Christmas and Easter}.

Cartridge Disk A plastic or metal rigid container that protects disk.

Cassa *(It.)* A large drum.

Cassette A rigid case containing a magnetic tape which is used to input/output information (voice, music, etc.) using *Analog* wave form (see *Cartridge Disk).*

Cassette Ministudios (see *Ministudio).*

Castagnet, Castagnetta *(It.)* **Castagnettes** *(Fr.)* **Castagnole** *(Spa.)* **Castanheta** *(Por.)* Castanets. Clappers shaped liked spoons used in dancing.

Catch A humorous canon or round for several voices. The parts are so contrived that when the singers catch up each other's words, a different meaning is given.

Cavatina *(It.)* Cavatine *(Fr.)* A song of one part. Usually shorter than an aria, which it sometime precedes.

CBL, see *CAI.*

C clef A clef sign used to show the pitch of middle C. It is used for the Soprano, Alto and Tenor (see *Clef).*

CD A Compact Disk that was developed by Philips and Sony in 1982. It is easy to handle and compact size. The non contact read mechanism uses laser with a lack of signal deterioration combine to provide dense stable storage.

CD-DA A Compact Disk with Digital Audio was designed for storing music and formed the basis for various other related standards which include:

> *CD-ROM* (Read only Memory), a computer storage medium.
>
> *CD-ROM XA,* which simultaneously handles text, music and images.
>
> *CD-1* (interactive), an interactive medium which handles text, music and images for use in the home.
>
> Recordable CD, Orange Book
>
> *Orange Book issues in 1991 for CD family formats.*
>
> *Part One defines describes CD-MO (magneto-optical disk) that can be written over any number of times.*
>
> *Part Two defines CD-WO (write once) that can be written once, but data added sequentially until the disk is full. The Orange Book specifications differ from others, such as those for C-ROM and CD-1 in the "Yellow Book" and the "Green Book" in that they define a format for recordable media.*
>
> *A dedicated drive is needed to read data from a CD-MO disk, but CD-WO, also known as CD-R (recordable), is a format for recording data so that it can be read by the same ordinary drives as are used for the CD-ROM or CD-DA. This compatibility and the ability to store vast amounts of data gives CD-R the potential for a wide range of uses.*
>
> *Orange Book Part 2 Modes*
>
> *Disk-at-once mode is designed for recording the whole disc at once and not adding data later.*
>
> *Track-at-once mode allows for stopping after recording only part off the disc, then adding further data later, but not reading from the disk until the fixation data is finally added.*
>
> *Multisession mode allows for stopping after recording only part of the disc, reading the disc, and adding further data to the unused part of the disc. This can be repeated until there is no recording space left on the disk, then it can be used in the read-only mode.*

CDEV *Control Panel Device* that allows user to set preferences for Macintosh system utilities such as a mouse speed and speaker volume.

CD-ROM XA refers to *Compact Disk Read Only Memory Extended Architecture* is like the CD-I in that the storage disc combines computer text and graphics with still image video information along with high quality audio.

CDTV plays audio and video programs from a disk. It can store 300,000 pages of typed text or 7000 video images which would be equivalent to the storage capacity of 1,000 floppy disks. This is an outgrowth of the digital audio compact disk, the *CD-ROM.*

C dur *(Ger.)* Key of C major.

Celesta Instrument with a piano keyboard which strikes a mallet on steel tuning forks.

'Cello *(It.)* Abb. of Violoncello.

Cembalo *(It.)* A Harpsichord.

Ceramic Microphone, see *Piezoelectric Microphone.*

Ces *(Ger.)* The note, *C flat.*

Ces dur *(Ger.)* The key of C flat major.

Chacona *(Spa)* **Chaconne** *(Fr.)* A slow dance in $3/4$ time. It is composed on a ground bass and Spanish in character.

Chamber Music. Music composed for performance in a room or a small hall by a small instrumental group.

Changing notes. A passing note on the accented part of a measure.

Channel-Stealing-Algorithm, see *Algorithm.*

Chanson *(Fr.)* A song.

Chant A short composition, usually a simple melody that is harmonized in four parts. Its text is usually of a religious nature.

Chart See *Arrangement, Score, Orchestration.*

Chase *(Fr.)* In a hunting style.

Chiarentana *(It.)* Italian country dance.

Chiarezza *(It.)* Clear, neat, pure.

Chime Sound of bells in harmony.

Chitarra *(It.)* A guitar.

Chiuso *(It.)* Close, hidden.

Choir A group of singers. Part of a cathedral or church set apart for the singers.

Choir Organ is a portion of the organ set apart containing a corresponding manual with softer sounds.

Choral Music, either sacred or secular, written or arranged for a mixed choral group, usually *Soprano, Alto, Tenor and Bass* (S.A.T.B.)

Chorale *(Ger.)* Hymn tunes of the early German Protestant church.

Chord The combination of two or more sounds heard at the same time. It is either consonant or dissonant.

Chord, common A chord consisting of its fundamental note together with the third and fifth.

Chord, dominant A chord that is found on the fifth degree of the scale in which the music is written.

Chord, inverted The lowest tone is not the root or fundamental. It may be the third, fifth, seventh, ninth, eleventh or thirteenth.

Chorus A group of singers. A composition to be sung by a number of voices. In the ancient Greek days the chorus was a group of singers and dancers.

Chorusing is a modulation effect as pitch shifting. It is extremely small as a millisecond. It is where two sounds or signals go in and out of tune (See *Modulation).*

Chromatic Includes notes that do not belong to the diatonic scale.

Chromatic scale A scale that divides every whole tone in the diatonic scale into twelve semitones which are half steps.

Chromatic signs, See *Accidentals.*

Chromatic Transposition, see *Transposition.*

Ciaccona, Ciacconne *(It.)* See Chacona.

Cis *(Ger.)* The note C sharp.

Cis-cis *(Ger.)* The note C double sharp.

Cis dur *(Ger.)* The key of C sharp major.

Cis moll *(Ger.)* The key of C sharp minor.

Clam, Clamour are terms applied to bell ringing, to unite sounds and a rapid multiplication of strokes.

Clarinet A rich full toned wind instrument made of wood, plastic or metal. It has a single reed mouthpiece.

Clarino is a shrill toned narrow tubed trumpet. This name may be given to an ordinary trumpet or bugle. It is also a reed stop in an organ, usually a 4-foot pitch.

Clarionet refers to a clarinet.

Classical music Music of a standard nature that has lived through many years, developed and written by masterful composers of the past. Some of our popular music dating beyond 1900 that have stood up to time are called standards.

Clavecin *(Fr.)* The harpsichord or spinet.

Clavichord A small stringed, keyboard instrument, the forerunner of the piano.

Clavier *(Fr. and Ger.)* Keyboard. A name given to keyboard instruments.

Clef The character set at the beginning of the staff to determine the name and pitch of the notes.

Treble Clef　　Alto Clef　　Tenor Clef　　Bass Clef

Click Track are timed beats, similar to the *clicks* or *beats* of a metronome. These can be recorded on one track on a multi-track recording which are used to synchronize additional tracks of live performances and with movie films. These audio tracks may be recorded on tape or on a MIDI Sequencer.

Clipboard Temporary holding place that facilitates the cutting and pasting of text and graphics. Music and text may be stored.

Clock A source of timing information. This is important when two or more devices must be synchronized.

Close A cadence, the end of a piece or passage.

Close harmony Harmony where the notes or parts are kept as close together as possible.

C moll *(Ger.)* The key of C minor.

Coaxial cable is capable of transmitting a high-quality. Modulated signals require a transmitter and receiver.

Coda *(It.)* "Tail" The end. It may be a section added at the end of a piece for a more dramatic ending.

Codetta *(It.)* A short coda or passage added to a piece.

Col arco *(It.)* With the bow.

Coll' arco *(It.)* played with a bow.

Col' legno *(It.)* With the bow stick.

Colla déstra *(It.)* With the right hand.

Colla parte *(It.)* With the principal part.

Colla sinistra *(It.)* With the Left Hand.

Colla voce *(It.)* With the voice.

Coll' ottava *(It.)* With the octave. Add the octave to the printed note.

Colofónia *(It.)*, **Colophane** *(Fr.)*, **Colophonium** *(Lat.)*, Colophony is *Rosin*, that is used for rubbing the hair on bows to produce resistance to vibrate strings on bowed instruments.

Coloratúra *(It.)* **Colorature** *(It.)* **Coloraturen** *(Ger.)* Ornamental passages, embellishments that are used to indicate a voice capable of executing florid passages.

Come Il primo tempo *(It.)* In the same time as the first.

Come prima *(It.)* As before; as at first.

Cóme sópra *(It.)* As before; as above. Repetition of a previous or similar passage.

Commódo *(It.)* Quiet and easily with composure.

Cómodo *(It.)* Quietly without rushing.

Common chord A chord consisting of a bass note with its third and fifth.

Common measure A measure that has an even number of parts. It usually refers to 4/4 rhythm which is sometimes marked C.

Como tempo del tema *(It.)* In the same time as the theme.

Compass The range of notes or sounds of which any voice or instrument is capable of producing.

Composite Vocal Tracks are constructed by submixing several chosen performances to a single track. It is necessary to have several open tracks to record a number of vocal takes, called a *bouncing of tracks*. Automatic mixing can be a great help in this.

Composition A musical production. Art of composing.

Compound harmony Harmony with an octave added.

Compound intervals Intervals which exceed an octave; as ninth, tenth, eleventh.

Compound stops Where three or more organ stops are used by pressing one key, all sound at once.

Compound time Those measures which include or exceed six parts, and contain two or more principle accents, as $6/4$, $9/4$, $6/8$, $9/8$, and $12/8$.

Computer Aided Instruction, see *CAI*.

Computer Based Learning, see *CAI*.

Computer Music is created directly into a computer through a software program with the use of a *Keyboard* or a *Mouse.*

Computer Music Systems *(CMS)*A point-of-purchase that utilize a NoteStation in a music store. It is sheet music on demand by a customer. Some music stores have this Music Source in the store, which takes about seven square feet of space. Music publishers give the rights out for certain fees, thus they are compensated along with the composer/author. The music is printed, according to title and composer, with the key desired, on a Laser Printer with a 300 dots per inch (dpi) resolution on plain or bond paper. This will be minus the attractive covers. An advantage of this would be the music store would not have to carry large inventories of music. For the buyer it is instant music in any key desired. Music programs transpose immediately when the desired key is programmed in.

Compressor smooths the level of an input signal by regulating the dynamic level. It prevents the signal from exceeding or falling below the acceptable range. Usually it attenuates high level signals.

Con *(It.)* With.

Concert-meister *(Ger.)* The chief violinist of the orchestra and leader of the violin section.

Concerto *(It.)* A composition in three movements which displays a solo instrument, usually with orchestra accompaniment.

Condenser microphone picks sounds by a charged metallic diaphragm. This is separated by a conductive back plate by a layer of air. It also contains a battery as a power source.

Conductor A director or leader of an orchestra or chorus.

Con Expressione *(It.)* Execute with expression according.

Consecutive fifths Two of the same parts moving together, a perfect fifth apart. In the study of traditional harmony this was not allowed.

Consecutive octaves Two of the same parts moving together, a perfect octave apart. In traditional harmony this was not allowed.

Console Refers to an organ with its manuals (keyboards) and pedals. It also refers to a display terminal which consists of a keyboard and monitor.

Contact Pickup Microphones are usually attached to an acoustical instrument. It is a very small mic.

Contano *(It.)* This indicates that in certain parts, the instruments remain silent, thus the performer counts the rest measures while the orchestra keeps playing.

Contra *(It.)* Low, under.

Contra-bass *(It.)*, Contra-basso *(It.)*, Contra-bass viol. The double bass; the deepest or lowest toned stringed instrument played with a bow.

Contra-bassoon Sometimes called the double bassoon, is deepest and lowest instrument of the bassoon family. It has a double reed mouthpiece.

Contractor One in a supervisory position of hiring, coaching, conducting, re-arranging, correcting music.

Contracts Agreements of understanding between two or more parties. In the music industry it could be a contract between a songwriter and publisher. This would be for original material. The publisher can save the writer(s) much time in dealing with business matters and make sure the right connections are established. Others could be between a major recording company, writers and performers. It is possible the company may advance funds, to set up a business venture, record an album and send the artist(s) on tour. An Independent label contract may be a cooperative agreement where artist pays all recording costs and the independent takes care of the pressing and distribution. In reference to a Production contract, independent producers sign with an artist or writer and promotes the artist and original material. There can be many variables.

Contralto *(It.)* The lowest female voice, usually called *alto.*

Controller Is what a person plays (musical information) on a musical instrument that transmits performance information as *MIDI* data. This would relate to drum pads, the keyboard, wind or brass instruments. The MIDI controller sends this musical information to another device that uses MIDI language being an instrument, module, computer, percussion pads, a wind instrument, sequencer or most any electrical or digital structures that uses the MIDI language. Manual controllers may be operated by the hands and feet. These controllers may be wheels, sliders, foot switches and volume footpedals.

Controller Data refers to a numerically MIDI code. This carries variable performance information when played. It is sometimes called *continuous controller data.*

Controller Numbers refers to MIDI locations for contact with controller data as to loudness, sustain pedal, pitch, modulation. The numbers applied depend on the users software.

Controls may refer to melody or Solo Sections; Drum and Rhythmic Sounds; Playing Mode Controls as to Fingered Chords, 1-finger chord, Manual; bass and or Automatic Bass Chords.

Control Track refers to the lower portion of a tape where all the sync information is recorded.

Copy Format is a way of preparing the disk for usage by organizing the tracks and sectors.

Copyright Notice "©" is a warning sign that information is protected by U.S. & International copyright law. The symbol for this is placed before the name of the copyright owner, with the current date.

Copyrights are enforceable by the U.S. Copyright Act. Rules have been changed since March 1, 1989, where it has been implied that the © symbol no longer has to be used. Use it, with date and your name and register all your important work(s) with the Copyright Office, Library of Congress, Washington, D.C. 20559. This is your proof to ownership. The U.S. became a member of the International Copyright Treaty on the above date.

Corda *(It .)* A string.

Corne *(Fr.)* A horn.

Cornet A brass instrument with three valves for the production of the chromatic scale. It is similar to a trumpet but shorter in length.

Corno *(It.)* A horn.

Coro *(It.)* A choir or piece for many voices.

Cosmetic Glove Using a *myoelectric* (muscle electric) model of a cosmetic glove, containing a tiny electric motor, one can actuates finger motion. Electrical impulses created by contractions of the forearm muscles, or *remnants* of the amputated muscle, are picked up by electrodes worn on the forearm and connected to an electronic amplifier (contained in a small box) which controls the miniature motor in the cosmetic glove. Thus a person who has lost a hand(s) can actually render tasks previously done as playing a keyboard instrument.

Counter A name given to a part sung or played against another.

Counterpoint "Point against point". Before notes were invented sounds were expressed by *points.* Added points either above or below are called *counterpoints* In our day, it is a support of the melody by another melody instead of chords.

Courante *(Fr.)* An old dance in triple time. It is of a rapid tempo.

Crash is an unexpected stoppage of the computer functioning that may destroy information. This is one important reason why data should be saved while entering information of any kind.

Credits refer to title, subtitles, name of author(s), screen writer(s), director, producers, cameramen, costume designer, location manager, composers, arrangers, casting director(s).

Crescendo *(It.)* A swelling, increasing the power of tone.

Cross Fade refers to a sound or a picture fading out while the next sequence fades over it.

Crotchet. *(Eng.)* A Quarter note.

Crystal Microphone, see *Piezoelectric Microphone.*

C Sound is a program used in computer music programming (see *Unix Operating System).*

Cue A selection of music used in a film or video that can range from a short piece of background music to a more complex selection.
The last words of an actor on stage as a guide to those that follow.
Small notes giving a phrase as a guide to those making an entry after a rest.

Cut, Copy and Paste is moving something from one place in a document to another. It can be the same document or a different one. This applies to music as well, notation and sound. It is most useful for editing as it can be temporary until one decides to save.

Cycle or Cyclical forms The Sonata, Symphony, String Quartet, Suite are examples of this because of being made up of several complete movements and forms.

Cymbals Circular brass plates which are set in vibration by being clashed together, or struck with a mallet causing a ringing sound.

D

D The second note in the diatonic scale of C. The key having two sharps in its signature.

Da *(It.)* From, by, about, of, for.

Da camera *(It.)* Style of chamber music.

Da cápo *(It.)* From the beginning; used at the end of a movement to indicate that the player is to return to the first strain. In such a case, repeats indicated by dots are generally not made after D.C.

Da cápo al fíne *(It.)* Return to the beginning and end at *fine.*

Da cápo al segno *(It.)* Repeat from the sign

𝄋

Da cápo e poi la coda *(It.)* Begin again and play to the coda.

Da cápo senza replica *(It.)* without repetition.

Dal, Dall', Dalla, Dalle, Dallo *(It.)* From the; by the; for the.

Dal segno *(It.)* from the sign.

Damper A portion of wood with felt for stopping the vibration of a string. A mute.

Damper pedal The *right* pedal of the piano which lifts the dampers from the strings.

DAT An acronym for **D**igital **A**udio **T**ape. It is a digital tape-recorder format that holds about two hours of 16 bit, linear pulse-code recorder. It encodes, transmits and stores digital information. These are becoming a standard for professionals. It looks like a small VHS tape claimed to give perfect recording (see *Digital Tape Modular Digital Multitracks).*

Data can be either *Input* or *Output* and can be any information such as graphics, letter and number characters, music. This is usually done on the keyboard. It is processed information.

DAWs, see *Digital Audio Workstations.*

D.C., see *Da capo.*

D dur *(Ger.)* D major.

dBmV stands for decibels referenced to 1 millivolt It is based on a logarithm of the ratio between a signal voltage and 1 millivolt(0.001 volts). dBmV is usually found as a reference value associated with modulating and demodulating equipment.

Decani *(Lat.)* On the side of the Dean. The Decani side in a cathedral choir is where the dean sits.

Decay The gradual diminishing of a sound after the original attack. (see *ASDR).*

Deceptive cadence Instead of a cadence closing on the tonic when preceded by the dominant, it closes with a chord, usually foreign to the harmony of the tonic.

Decibel is a measure of *(dB)* sound or loudness.

Decimal, see *Hexadecimal.*

Decisivo *(It.)* **Deciso** *(It.)* In a bold and decided manner.

Declamando *(It.)* In a declamatory manner.

Decr., **Decres.**, **Decrescendo** *(It.)* Diminishing in power of tone.

Degree The step between two tones. It may be a half-tone *(minor second)* or a whole tone *(major second)* or a tone and a half *(augmented second)* The intervals may vary.

Del *(It.)* Of the.

Delicatissimo *(It.)* Delicately.

Demi *(Fr.)* Half.

Demo *A* demonstration recording of a song, sounds. Also a program for audition purposes and getting it ready for marketing purposes. A non-air commercial, generally recorded for client approval.

Des dur *(Ger.)* D flat major. Dos. D flat.

Des moll *(Ger.)* Key of D flat minor.

Desto *(It.)* Brisk, sprightly.

Destra *(It.)* Right. Destra mano, the right hand.

Détaché *(Fr.)* Detached, staccato.

Determinatíssimo, Determináto, Determinazióne *(It.)* Determined, resolute.

Détonnation *(Fr.)* False intonation.

Detto *(It.)* The same.

Deutlich *(Ger.)* Distinctly.

Deux *(Fr.)* Two.

Development The elaboration of a theme.

Devóto *(It.)* Devout, religious.

Di *(It.)* Of, with, for, from, to.

Dia *(Ger.)* Through, throughout.

Diapason *(Lat., Gr. and Eng.)* The whole octave. The compass of a voice or instrument. The English name of the organ stops which the Italians and Germans call principal. The Diapasons are the most important foundation of organs stops.

Diatonic *(Ger.)* Proceeding in the order of degrees of the natural scale, including tones and semi-tones.

Diatonic major scale. The semi-tones come between the third and fourth, seventh and eighth degrees, both in ascending and descending.

Di chiaro *(It.)* Clearly.

Diese *(Fr.)* A sharp (see *Accidentals*).

Diese, double *(Fr.)* A double sharp (see *Accidentals*).

Di gala *(It.)* Merrily, cheerfully.

Digital is where data is stored as numbers which represent discrete points on a waveform (example: a Digital keyboard or a piano). Recording would be a maximum signal or nothing at all. Selecting a Television Station is a digital process as only a specific channel can be used and nothing in between, as 3.5. It has to be either 3 or 4. A Digital system counts discrete units in comparison to a Analog system which would mean over a continuous range or waves. In the Digital System all output and input by a computer is made up of two voltages levels "0" and "1" (see *Digit*).

Digital Audio A recording technique that stores sound (see *ADC*).

Digital Audio Workstations Hard disk recording is becoming quite common as used at home an in various aspects of the business doing music work and production. It is a tapeless recording machine that edits, plays back, and mixes.

Digital Compact Cassette An equivalent to the analog cassette with the addition of search features along with a digital display.

Digital Film Recorder Reads files from graphic software and converts the digital data into an analog signal.

Digitally Controlled Amplifier (DCA) An amplifier circuit where an output gain can be varied by a digital signal.

Digitally Controlled Oscillator (DCO) Refers to an Oscillator circuit where an output frequency can be varied by a digital signal.

Digital Phase Modulation, see *DPM.*

Digital Piano contains an electric keyboard with features of an acoustical piano which include weighted keys, touch sensitivity with attached pedals. Usually have built-in speakers and audio inputs and outputs for use with other sources.

Digital Recording is another way of recording that involves a sequence of pulsation, or *on-off* signals rather than the continuous variable analog signal. This provides for a greater frequency range and lower tape noise.

Digital Sampling is a process of obtaining sounds. Usually the process is made by an original instrument, converting its sounds into an electrical wave by a microphone, converting these samples to numbers, storing the numbers in memory, the numbers are converted into sound by a converter, a filter smooths out and refines the sound and the sound is then transmitted through an amplifier and speaker (see *A to D*).

Digital Tape Modular Digital Multitracks (MDMs) A MDM makes an easier transition to digital recording than a hard-disk recorder. It is not analog tape. On a digital deck, tracks are converted into digital data and thus laid down to tape in a series of packets. The tape must be formated like a floppy disk. There are three formats: DAT, S-VHS which is employed by the Alesis ADAT and the Fostex RD-8) and the Hi-8 used by Tascam's DA-88. It uses the Binary language of the computer, the *ones and zeroes.* The heads are tilted creating the effect of a high tape speed. More data is also held in this format than an analog tap. To prevent pirating one cannot make a digital copy of a digital which puts a composer at a disadvantage, in case the original master gets damaged. Therefore a composer should obtain a pro DAT recorder, the professional AES/EBI digital inputs and outputs as the SCMS are not recognized.

Digital-to-analog converter *(DAV)* converts audio from a digital format to an analog signal.

Digital Transmission A data communication that passes information as on-off pulses in opposition to a continuous wave length (see *Analog, Digital*).

Diligenza *(It.)* Diligent and careful.

Diluendo *(It.)* A gradual dying away of a tone until it is extinct.

Diminished Made less.

Diminished interval Those intervals which are a semitone less than a minor of perfect interval.

Diminuendo *(It.)* Same as *Decrescendo;* diminishing the intensity or power of tone gradually.

Di molto *(It.)* Very much.

Direct Voice Input When one uses the voice to control the computer.

Dis *(Ger.)* D sharp.

Disaccentato *(It.)* Unaccented.

Di salto *(It.)* By leaps or by skips.

Discant The upper part.

Discord A combination of unharmonious, dissonant sounds.

Dis moll *(Ger.)* Key of D sharp minor.

Disk A magnetically coated platter that stores programs and data files. The two main type of disks are hard disks and floppy disks. These must be Initialized (formated) before using.

Disk Array Music notation and sounds take over much storage space on computers. A way of overcoming this is the Disk Array with a collection of individual hard disk drives connected or stringed together controlled by one computer.

Disk Drive is used for disks that store programs, backups and other types of data. Information can be stored on a double density (DD) disk or a high density disk (HD). Each disk must be formated to the computer or keyboard before being used. Each appliance would have its own formatted disk.

Divisi *(It.)* Divided, separated.

Divoto *(It.)* In a solemn style.

D moll *(Ger.)* Key of D minor.

Do *(It.)* A syllable applied to the first note of the scale. In the *'fixed Do'* system, *'C'* is always *Do*. In the 'movable *Do* system, it always represents the keynote, whether that note is *C* or not.

Doctor of Music is the highest music degree confirmed by universities.

Dolby contains noise reduction circuitry. The popular ones are Dolby B and C for cassettes only. Dolby A and Dolby SR are expensive in comparison. Dolby found a way to squeeze a 4-channel soundtrack in the same space on a film print, the size of a mono track. Two narrow optical tracks optical tracks were used for the main left and right channels and encoding them with two additional tracks, center and surround, using a matrixing process that was similar to the quadraphonic home-stero format. On the playing of the film, a Dolby Stereo decoder reads the two encoded optical tracks and extracts the four original signals and directs them to the various amplifiers and speakers.

Dolce *(It.)* Sweetly, softly, delicately.

Dolce con gusto *(It.)* Soft and sweet, with taste and expression.

Dolce e cantabile *(It.)* Sweet, soft in a singing style.

Dolcissimo *(It.)* with extreme sweetness and delicacy.

Dolente *(It)* Sorrowful, mournful, pathetic.

Dominant The name given to the fifth note of the scale.

Dominant chord A chord constructed on the fifth note of the scale.

Dominant seventh chord A minor seventh interval, from the root (fifth note of the scale) added to the dominant chord.

Dónna *(It.)* The principal female singer in an opera.

Donut A jingle format where the vocals are placed at the beginning and end with the instrumental part in the middle which would include the voice-over with the *sell* message.

Dópo *(It.)* After.

Doppio *(It.)* Double; twofold; sometimes indicating that octaves are to be played. **Dóppio moviménto** *(It.)* indicates double movement, twice as fast.

Doppio pedale *(It.)* a bass passage on organ with the pedals moving in octaves. This is usually done with both feet. There are some contemporary organs that will do this automatically.

Doppler Shift A sound created as a moving vehicle comes toward *you* and passes *you,* there will be a drop in pitch (see *Modulation).*

Dot A mark (dot) when placed after a note increases its value by half. When the dot is placed over or under a note it is to be played staccato, crisp, about one half of the notes value (see *Detached, Gestossen, Staccato).*

Dots When placed at the side of a bar line or double bar line shows that the music on that side is to be repeated (see *Bar, Double).*

Double bar Two vertical lines drawn through the staff at the end of a section, movement, or a portion to be repeated (see *Bar, Double).*

Double bass The largest and deepest-toned instrument played with a bow or plucked. An electronic bass is now being made which is much smaller in size.

Double flat A character placed before a note lowers the note a whole step which is two semi-tones (see *Accidentals).*

Double fugue A fugue with two subjects.

Double octave A fifteenth, the interval of two octaves.

Double quartet A composition written for eight voices or eight instruments.

Double reed The mouthpiece of the Oboe, Bassoon formed of two pieces of cane joined together.

Double sharp A character which raises a note a whole step, two semi-tones (see *Accidentals).*

Doubling A performer playing more than one instrument.

Doucement *(Fr.)* Sweetly, softly, pleasingly.

Douleur *(Fr.)* Grief, sorrow, pathos.

Doux *(Fr.)* Sweet, soft, gentle.

Down beat The first beat or count to a measure.

Download Act of transferring files from one computer to another or of loading fonts from a computer to a printer.

Doxology A song or hymn of praise.

DPM *Digital Phase Modulation* which is a sample playback using digital filters.

Dramatic Performance Rights, see *Grand Rights.*

Dritta *(It.)*, **Dritto** *(It.)* Right. Mano dritta, the right hand.

Droite *(Fr.)* Right, Main droite, the right hand.

Drop In Refers to a speck of dirt or foreign matter on a tape (see *Drop Out).*

Drop Out A loss of recorded data during a playback because of imperfections in a tape or some dirt on the surface of a tap.

Drum A percussion instrument, with skin or parchment on both sides of a cylinder of wood, metal, or plastic.

Drum Set Different percussive sounds are assigned to different individual notes/keys on the keyboard. This makes the possibility of playing drum solos on the keys.

Drum Sounds indicate Rhythm styles as $3/4$, $4/4$, Bossa Nova, Country, Disko, Rock, Slow Rock, and others. Supplementary controls added to these may be Arpeggio, Fill In and Intro/Ending, Start/Stop, Tempo, Variation and Volume.

D. S. Abbreviation of *Dal Segno.*

Dub Copying a tape.

Dubbing Technique of transcribing a sound track from one recording medium to another.

Ducking A term used in lowering the volume of music when one desires a voice or lead instrument to stand out.

Due corde *(It.)* Two strings.

Duet *(It.)*, **Duo** *(Fr.)* Duetto *(It.)* A composition for two voices or instruments, or for two performers on one instrument.

Duple, Double, Duple time Two beats to a measure.

Dur *(Ger.)* Major.

Dynamic Microphone transforms sound, acoustic energy, into electrical voltage to a loudspeaker thus converting it back to a louder acoustic degree. In reality it is a speaker that works backwards. It is often called a *moving coil mic.*

Dynamics This term has reference to expression and the loudness and softness of the tone(s) to be used.

E

E In France and Italy it is called *mi*, the third note in the scale of C.

E, Ed *(It.)* And.

EBU Time Code is the *European Broadcast Union* version of SMPTE time code (see *SMPTE).*

Echo A repetition, or imitation of a previous passage of music, softer in tone than the previous or original notes. On electronic organs it is a sound held over slightly by reverberation.

Ecossais *(Fr.)*, **Ecossaise** *(Fr.)* A Scottish dance tune done in a lively tempo.

Edit To make changes by cutting or splitting one scene to another.

E dur *(Ger.)* Key of E major.

EG's, see *Envelope, Modulation.*

Eighth An octave, an interval of eight diatonic degrees.

Eighth Note Triplet Three eighth notes played in the value of two (see *Tuplets*).

Ein or **Eine** *(Ger.)* A, an, one.

Eis *(Ger.)* The note E sharp.

Eisis *(Ger.)* E double sharp.

Electret Microphones Uses a static charge and is powered by an internal transistor amplifier. The smallness of these units can be used in extremely close situations.

Electric musical instruments Uses electrical means for reproducing acoustical sounds by microphones that capture the vibrations of the instrument. Examples of this would be the electric guitar, violin, trumpet, or any acoustic instrument.

Electric Piano Voices are generated through the digital process (see *Envelope).*

Electromagnetic waves Also called radiation, occur at different frequencies that include radio frequencies *(RF)*, microwaves, infrared heat, visible light, x-rays and gamma rays.

Electronic musical instrument A music device that uses electronic circuits to create sounds which would include many keyboards, organs, synthesizers and samplers.

Elegamment *(Fr.)* **Elegantemente** *(It.)* **Elegante** *(It.)*

Eleganza *(It.)* Elegance, graceful.

Elegia *(It.)* **Elegie** *(Fr.)* An elegy.

Elegy Music of a mournful character.

Embellishment Decorations as a trill, mordent, turn, grace notes.

Embouchure *(Fr.)* The position of the lips on the mouthpiece to produce a tone on a wind instrument.

E moll *(Ger.)* Key of E minor.

Emulate The imitation, or duplication of certain characteristics of one device while using another. Many sequencers can emulate multi-track tape recorders.

En *(Fr.)* In.

Endless Loop A tape that keeps repeating itself until turned off. There is no ending piece on this kind of tape. This is used a great deal in answering machines attached to a telephone.

Energetico *(It.)* **Energia** *(It.)* **Energie** *(Fr.)* Energy, force, emphasis.

Enfatico *(It.)* Emphatic with earnestness.

English fingering. "x" is used in piano music to designate the thumb rather than the figure "1".

English horn Cor Anglais *(Fr.)* A double reed instrument sounding a fifth lower than the oboe.

Engraver spacings are specified by rules in laying out a page of music with placement of notes, lyrics and symbols. When a half note takes up as much horizontal spacing as a quarter note, it is known as linear spacing. Rules set down by engravers determine a non-linear spacing format based on the music context. A half note would get less than twice the space of a quarter note. The Lyric text should fit comfortably with the music notation.

Enharmonic Used in modern music, it is a change in the writing of a note without changing the pitch. Example: C sharp, D flat; G flat, F sharp.

Enharmonic transposition, see *Transposition.*

Ensemble *(Fr.)* All together.

Entr'acte *(Fr.)* Music played between the acts of a drama.

Envelope A vibration wave form that represents the dynamics of tone *(ADSR or ASDR).* This provides the parameters which the user can vary the sounds or shapes of softness to loudness and the timbre and pitch. Each tone should have the following: *Attack, Final Release, Initial Decay, Peak, Sustain Level, Time* and *Volume.* Some instruments have a rapid or sharp attack with a rapid decay as a piano and drums. Strings, reeds and brass instruments have a long sustained level. The Envelope Generator *(EG's)* in early generations only had the attack, decay, sustain and release segments. It is now normal or possible to have more than two-hundred segments in an envelope.

Envelope Generator, see *Envelope.*

Episode An accessory part to a composition.

EQ refers to equalization as to correct placement of instruments that will give a great sound without muddiness, hiss, distortion, pops, crackles along with other noises. Strive for a clean recording.

Equalization, see *EQ.*

Erase Head refers to the separate head on an audio or videotape recorder which erases a previous taped signal before it is reprogrammed.

Error A mistake of some kind.

Es *(Ger.)* E flat.

Es dur *(Ger.)* E flat major.

Es moll *(Ger.}* E flat minor.

Espressione (lt.), **Espressivo** *(lt.)* With expression.

Etude *(Fr.)* A study; a lesson.

Euphonium The modern Baritone horn, a wind instrument usually used in bands.

Expander attenuates low-level signals. Usually it masks unwanted noise. See *Compresser, Ducking, Gates, VCA.*

Explode Music Takes a chordal piece of music, written on two staves, and converts it into several individual lines of melody on separate staves.

Expression A term used to express personal feeling and taste in playing music.

Expressivo *(lt.)* With expression and feeling.

Extemporize To improvise.

Extract Parts To copy a part from an orchestral score and place on an individual staff for a specified instrument.

F

F The fourth tone of the diatonic major scale of C. It is called *Fa* in France and Italy.

Facile *(Fr. and lt.)* Light and easy.

Fade A gradual increase or decrease of audio or video signal. In a video system it is the gradual appearance of an image from black or vice versa. In audio and music, it means decreasing the present or full volume to a lesser volume, even down to zero volume.

Fade In refers to a gradual increase in volume in MIDI instruments. See *Fade*.

Fade Out refers to a gradual decrease in volume in MIDI instruments. See *Fade*.

Fagott *(Ger.)* **Fagotto** *(lt.)* The Bassoon.

False accent When the accent is moved from the first beat of the measure to the second or fourth

False relation When a tone has been used in a chord is found chromatically changed in the following chord, but in a different part. Examples would be a *Cb* used for *B,* or *C#* used for *Db.*

Falsetto *(lt.)* A false or artificial voice. It is the part of a singer's voice that lies above its natural range.

Fanfare *(Fr.)* Usually a flourish of trumpets, or other loud instruments accompanied by drums.

Fantaisie *(Fr.)* **Fantasia** *(lt.)* **Fantasie** *(Ger.)* A composition of irregular form. It follows the imagination of the composer without any regard to any restricted form.

Fantastico *(It.)* **Fantastique** *(Fr.)* Fantastic, grotesque.

FCC is the abbreviation for the government agency, called *Federal Communications Commission.* This agency controls the use of airwaves for broadcasting purposes. The U.S.A. has over crowded airwaves with uses for most everything as radio, television, cellular phones, garage door openers. The National Telecommunications has proposed auctioning off these airwaves for broadcasting licenses to the highest bidder. From this the government could raise $3.4 billion for the U.S. Treasury and create a free market for the airwaves.

F clef The bass clef character placed on the fourth line of the staff with the two dots on the third and fourth spaces (see *Clef).*

F dur *(Ger.)* Key of F major.

Ferma *(It.)* **Fermamente** *(It.)* Firm, steady.

Fermáta *(It.)* **Fermate** *(Ger.)* A pause or hold. ⌢

Fermáte, Fermáto *(It.)* Firmly, steadily, resolutely.

Fermement, Fermeté *(Fr.),* **Fermézza, Férmo** *(It.)* Firm, resolute.

Feroce, Ferocemente, Ferocita *(It.)* Fierce.

Fervido *(It.)* Fervent, vehement.

Fes *(Ger.)* The note F flat.

Festivo *(It.)* Merry, cheerful, gay.

F holes The sound holes on a violin, or other stringed instrument.

Fife A small, shrill-toned instrument like a flute usually played with drums.

Fifteenth An interval of two octaves.

Fifth A distance comprising three tones and a semi-tone *(Ger., Quinte; Fr., Quinte; It., Quinta.).*

Fifth, augmented An interval containing four whole tones. Sometimes called a Sharp fifth, or Raised fifth.

Figuration Ornamental treatment of a passage.

Figured bass A bass part with figures over or under the notes to indicate the harmony *(6* means 3rd in bass, *6/4,* 5th in bass).

Filter An audio signal that is altered by the removal of portions of sounds that will modify its characteristics of sounds. It redirects a signal. In the computer, using certain programs with text matter or illustrations, according to filters applied, certain selected data may be extracted.

Fin *(Fr.)* The end.

Finale *(It.)* Final; the conclusion. The name of music software program put out by Coda for printing music notation.

Fine *(It.)* To show the end of a piece or movement after a repeat.

Fine Tune is the process of making very fine adjustments in a program to get the best results.

Fiorituri *(It.)* Little graces and ornaments in vocal music.

First inversion   When the bass takes the third of a chord.

Fis *(Ger.)* The note F sharp. *Fis-is*, F double sharp.

Fis moll *(Ger.)* Key of F sharp minor.

F Key pertaining to a MIDI Keyboard, or any keyboard, it would be the white key, preceding any three black keys.

Flanging is a modulation effect. The input signal (sound) is split into two copies. One copy is delayed by a varied amount of time, usually a milliseconds *(ms)* which is then mixed with the unprocessed signal (see *Modulation).*

Flat   Character placed before a note which lowers it one semi-tone (see *Accidentals, Chromatic signs).*

Flat double   Character placed before a note which lowers it a whole tone, two semi-tones   (see *Accidentals, Chromatic signs).*

Flat fifth   The diminished fifth   (°5), sometimes called lowered fifth.

Flat seventh   The minor seventh interval.

Fláuto *(It.)* a Flute

Florid   Embellished with runs, trills, and figures.

Flugelhorn *(Ger.)* A brass instrument similar to the cornet, but a little larger in size.

Flute   An instrument made of metal, sometimes wood closed at one end   (see *Instruments).*

Flutter echo   Sound bounced off of flat walls or sound reflections bouncing from wall to wall back and forth creating many echoes. It can also be caused by stairs and columns. To avoid this,   have sound absorbing ceiling, or walls, even a heavy carpet on the floor or other absorptive material would   help.

FM   The abbreviation for *Frequency Modulation* which is used in electronic sound. This wave form, applied to another effects a change, or a modulation in the pitch frequency. FM voices have the same physical sound characteristics as a real instrument. The FM sound wave(s) matches the shape(s) of an instrument(s) sound wave(s) and controls the complex harmonics when changed through the decay period (see *Envelope).*

F moll *(Ger.)* Key of F minor.

Foco *(It.)* Fire, ardor, passion. Also Fuoco.

Foot Switch can be at the *toe* part on the expression pedal of an electronic, or MIDI organ, either   left or right   sides,   or   both   sides. This   enables   the performer to stop rhythm, add a fill in pattern, increase the tempo. These must be programmed into the instrument before using. Other electronic instruments may also contain foot switches to obtain various sounds and effects.

Foreign Royalties   Revenues earned by songs performed outside the United States. Usually a sub publishing agreement is agreed upon with a foreign publisher who collects revenues within their territory.

Format To prepare a blank disk for receiving information by organizing its surface into tracks and sectors. It prepares the disk for future use. *NOTE: Usually each make of computer or keyboard has its own format. It requires a good filing system so disks are not misplaced or used in the wrong instrument. One can loose important material if not careful.*

Forte *(It.)* Loud, strong. Usually written *f*.

Forte-piano A piano. Sometimes called *Piano-forte.* It was given the combination of two name to let the interested person know it was capable of being played either soft or loud.

Fortissimo *(It.)* Very loud. Usually written *ff*.

Fortississimo *(It.)* As loud as possible. Usually written *fff*.

Forzato *(It.)* Laying stress on one chord or note.

Fourth An interval made from two tones and a half.

Fourth, augmented An interval containing three whole tones.

Freddo *(It.)* Cold, devoid of sentiment.

French Horn An orchestral horn with a wide flaring bell. It has a rich, mellow and sonorous sound. It has valves and is a transposing instrument pitched in F. The hand is put inside the bell at times to change the pitch of a note.

French sixth A form of an augmented sixth. It consists of the root, major third, augmented fourth and a augmented sixth. (Example: F#, A#, C and E.) In popular terminology it would sound as a C Seventh Chord with a flatted 5th (C7-5, C7°5 or C7b5).

Frequency The speed that cycles of a sound wave or electrical signals travel. The low, slower frequencies are the bass, and the high, faster frequencies are the treble. The rate of repetition is based on cycles per second.

Frequency Division Multiplexor *(FDM)* is a device that divides available transmission frequency range into narrower banks. Each one is for a separate channel.

Frequency Modulation (see *FM).*

Frequency Response The range in audio and video systems over which signals are reproduced in a standard dimensional range.

Frets Narrow strips of wood, ivory or wire, fixed on the fingerboards of the Guitar, Banjo, Mandolin to show where to place the fingers to produce various sounds.

Frog The handle of the violin bow. The tip is at the opposite end.

FSK Refers to *Frequency Shift Keying.* It is an audio sound or tone which is generated by a computer MIDI face or a sequencer, that is recorded on one track of an audio or video tape for synchronization to MIDI sequencers.

Fugue, Fuge *(Ger.),* **Fugha** *(It.)* It is a composition in strict style. A subject *(theme)* is given in one part and answered by other parts.

Full Organ An organ with all sounds or stops in use.

Fundamental The root of a chord.

Fundamental bass The name given to any bass note when the chord is constructed on that note.

Fundamental note The note on which the chord is constructed.

Fundamental tones The tonic, dominant and subdominant of any scale or key.

Funebre *(Fr.)*, **Funerale** *(It.)*, **Funereo** *(It.)* Funereal, mournful.

Furioso *(It.)* Furious and wild.

Furore *(It.)* Fury, rage, passion.

Fz. The abbreviation for *forzando* meaning force and accent.

G

G The fifth note in the diatonic scale of C. The letter name of the treble clef. The name of the key having one sharp in its signature. Also called *Sol*.

G *(Fr.)* Left; as "m. g." (With the left hand) (main gauche).

G dur *(Ger.)* Key of G major.

Gagliada *(It.)* A galliard.

Gagliardo *(It.)* Brisk, merry, gay.

Gai *(Fr.)* Gay, merry, brisk.

Gaiement or **Gaiment** *(Fr.)* Merrily, lively, gay.

Gaja or **Gajo** *(It.)* Gay, merry, lively.

Galliard A lively old dance in triple time. It is said to be of Italian origin.

Galop *(Fr.)* A lively dance in 2/4 time.

Gamma *(It.)*, Gamme (Fr.) The gamut or scale.

Gamut The scale of notes belonging to any key. Also the lines and spaces on which the notes are placed.

Garbage Unwanted, or meaningless material stored in a computer file whether it be text, music or graphics.

Gate or **Gating** Used to eliminate all noise when no signals are present.

Gauche *(Fr.)* Left.

Gavot *(Eng.)*, **Gavotta** *(It.)*, **Gavotte** *(Fr.)* An old dance of even rhythm usually in 4/4 time. (Sometimes *alla breve*, known as Cut Time " ¢ ." It should begin on the fourth beat.

Geige *(Ger.)* The violin.

Geist *(Ger.)* Spirit, soul, mind, genius.

General MIDI (GM) refers to an extension of MIDI specifications that established a set of program numbers for a variety of Synth sounds. These would include Piano: group 1-8, Chromatic Percussion: group 9-

16, Organ: group 17-24, Guitar: group 25-32, Bass: group 33-40, Strings: group 41-48, Ensemble: group 49-56, Brass: group 57-64, Reeds: group 65-72, Pipes: group 73-80, Synth Lead: group 81-88, Synth Pad: group 89-96, Synth Effects: group 97-104, Ethnic: group 105-112, Percussion and Drum Kits: group 113-120, and Sound Effects: group 121-128, Within this grouping, as an example 1 to 8 would be the Acoustic Grand Piano, Bright Acoust Piano, Electric Grand Piano, Honky-tonk Piano, Electronic Piano 1, Electronic Piano 2, Harpsichord and Clavichord. This would also apply to controllers as Velocity, Aftertouch and Sustain. The specifications would allow other GM compatible sequencer files to be played back through a GM system with known results. Patch #1 would always be a acoustic grand piano. Patch 25 is always a nylon stringed guitar. Patch #41 is always a solo violin. MIDI Channel #10 is reserved for rhythm and drum parts *(see MMA).*

Generations Refers to computer development. *First Generation* (using vacuum tubes), *Second Generation* (using Transistors), *Third Generation* (using intergrated circuits), *Fourth Generation* (using LSI and VISI circuits), and *Fifth Generation* (using easier technology, being able to understand the human voice, carrying a wealth of knowledge in relationship to CD-ROM). Beyond this, future generations will add to this as new technology steps into the picture.

German sixth. A form of an augmented sixth. It consists of the root, major third, perfect fifth and the augmented sixth. (Example: Gb, Bb, Db and E.)

Ges *(Ger.)* The note G flat.

Ges dur *(Ger.)* Key of G flat major.

Gestossen *(Ger.)* Separated, detached, staccato.

Getragen *(Ger.)* Sustained.

G gamut G on the first line of the bass staff.

Giga *(It.)* Gigue *(Fr.)* Gige *(Ger.)* A jig or lively dance.

Gioconda *(It.)* Cheerful, merry, gay.

Giocoso *(It.)* Humorously, sportively.

Gioja *(It.)* Joy, gladness.

Gis *(Ger.)* The note G sharp.

Gis moll *(Ger.)* Key of G sharp minor.

Gitana *(It.)* A Spanish dance.

Giubiloso *(It.)* Jubilation.

Giustezza *(It.)* Precision.

Giusto *(It.)* Equal, steady and exact time.

Glee A vocal composition in three of four parts, usually consisting of more than one movement.

Glide Portamento.

Glissando *(It.)* In a gliding manner.

Global Adjustment in a Music Notation Program is a time saving factor. If one is working on a page of music with certain attributes, and these differences are needed on all other pages, Global adjustment will take care of this. This is much simpler than manually changing each page to specifications as to note heads, style of notes, page layout and other important aspects.

Glocke *(Ger.)* A bell.

Glockenspiel *(Ger.)* A set of bells.

GM see *General MIDI.*

GM Bank see *General MIDI.*

G moll *(Ger.)* Key of G minor.

Grace-note A small note with an oblique line through the stem. It serves as an ornamental note played quickly (see *Acciaccatura).*

Gracieux *(Fr.)* Graceful.

Gracile *(It.)* Thin and weak. Refers to tone.

Gradazione *(It.)* By degrees.

Gran *(It.)* Grand *(Fr.)* Grande *(It.)* Large; great; full; complete.

Grandezza *(It.)* Grandeur and dignity.

Grandioso *(It.)* Grand and noble.

Grand jeux *(Fr.)* Full organ.

Grand Rights Dramatic performance rights which are the monetary earnings from works produced on Broadway, off Broadway as well as theatres throughout the country which includes plays, ballets, operas and other theatrical settings.

Graphic Display A display terminal that is designed for specialized applications as art, business, graphics, or music.

Graphic Equalizer Pertains to an audio device for adjusting the sound quality within a set frequency range.

Grappa *(It.)* The brace, or character used to connect two or staves.

Grave *(It.)* The slowest tempo in music. Also a deep low pitch in sound.

Gravita *(It.),* **Gravität** *(Ger.)* **Gravité** *(Fr.)* Gravity and majesty.

Gravity The modification of any sound when it becomes deep and low in respect to another sound.

Grazia, Grazioso *(It.)* Grazie *(Ger.)* Grace, elegance.

Great Organ If an organ has three manuals (three sets of keys), it is usually the middle row. This usually contains the most important stops with pipes voiced louder than those in the swell or choir organ.

Green Book, see *CD-DA.*

Gregorian chant A style of choral music introduced by Pope Gregory in the sixth century according to the eight church modes.

Grell *(Ger.)* Shrill, acute.

Grid is a page template, definition, containing predefined margins and columns. This also applies to manuscript paper.

Groppo, Gruppo, Gruppetto *(It.),* **Gruppe** *(Ger.)* Rapid note groups.

G-schlussel *(Ger.)* The treble or G clef.
Guitar A plucked six stringed instrument with a fretted fingerboard. It comes in various sizes, colors, combination of colors, and shapes, made from various materials. Strings used are gut, nylon, plain steel, stainless steel, nickel and phosphor bronze. Sounds are from acoustic to amplified, using pedals for effects.
Gusto *(It.)* Taste and expression.

H

H In the German system. *H* is used for *B* natural while *B* is used for *B* flat.
Haas Effect is derived from an experiment using human beings, who listened to two identical sounds with a very slight delay between them. The delay was increased until two distinct sounds were heard, rather than one. This psychoacoustic experiment plays a great part in creating effects on a MIDI instrument. For those in the active playing field one will find that the perfect beat is not always there. Even with a pianist or organist playing a full chord simultaneous it may sound together but it may not be.
Habanera *(Spa.)* A slow Spanish dance.
Halb *(Ger.)* Half.
Halb ton *(Ger.)* Half-tone, semi-tone.
Half-cadence An imperfect cadence; a close on the dominant.
Half-note A minum which has half the time value of a whole note, a semibreve.

Half Note Triplet

Half-rest Same duration as a Half-note.
Harmonica The modern Mouth-harp played by blowing and sucking the air through its reed holes. It may also be a set of musical glasses played by rubbing the edge of the glass with a finger.
Harmonic modulation A change in the harmony from one key to another.
Harmonic Series The first sound "C" is the fundamental, or the root frequency. The second sound "C" is one octave higher from the fundamental with the third sound "G" a Perfect Fifth higher than the "C." These harmonics produce a richness of tone. As an example, play the fundamental and listen closely. One will hear the "C" chord, C-E-G. For those with more sensitive hearing, one may hear the Bb which the fundamental sounds, thus creating the C7th Chord. If one plays the fundamental with the Damper pedal pressed down and held, one will set the audible overtone series into motion and actually hear them on an acoustical piano.

Harmonic Series

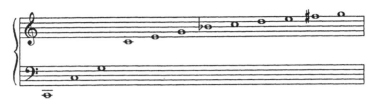

Harmonic Sounds are played on open strings as in violin or harp music. The mark "o' indicates the open string.

Harmonie *(Fr. and Ger.)* Harmony.

Harmonium A small reed organ.

Harmony The art of combining two or more sounds into chords.

Harmony, close Where the upper three voices are within the range of an octave.

Harmony, compound Harmony of another octave added.

Harmony, dispersed Harmony in which the notes forming different chords are separated by wide intervals.

Harp A string instrument of ancient origin. The modern harp has a system of double action pedals that can raise the pitch of a note either a semi-tone or a whole tone. It has forty-six strings usually and the C strings are colored red while the F strings are colored blue so that the performer can see the position of any note. A harp with a single action pedal will raise the pitch of each string one half step. Erard developed a harp with seven pedals in which the strings may be raised a semitone or a whole step and all keys would be practical. This double action harp has a span of about six and a half octaves, starting on Cb. The strings, usually made from cat gut, are plucked with the fingers of both hand to cause the sounds.

Harpsichord A keyboard stringed instrument, a forerunner of the piano. The strings are plucked by quills, leather and sometimes by a plastic material rather than being struck by hammers as a piano.

Harp, Jew's is a small instrument made from metal with a flexible metal tongue. By placing this instrument between the teeth and vibrating the tongue by striking it with the finger, the breathing action will determine the power of the tone.

Hashmark is the "#" used in the United States. It may precede a number as #1, #2, #3. In some programs the "#" is used for a number, and a number will appear when printed. It is also referred to as a *pound sign. Hashmarks* are also used in music to denote rhythmic notation to be played by guitar, ukulele, banjo, piano, and other rhythm instruments. It would also refers to the repetition of a chord *(/ / / /).*

Hautbois *(Fr.)* Hautboy *(Eng.)* The oboe.

Head tones are tones produced by the upper register of the voice.

Head-voice pertains to the upper or highest register of the voice. It would be the falsetto in men's voices.

H dur *(Ger.)* B major.

Hemidemisemiquaver *(Ger.)* Sixty-fourth note ♬ . Rest ♬

Heptachord relates to a system of seven sounds. Going back to ancient poetry, verses were sung or played on seven chords of different notes. It also refers to a either a cithera or lyre having seven strings.

Hexachord *(Ger.)* A scale or system of six sounds. Also a lyre having six strings. An interval of a sixth.

Hexadecimal (after Gr. Hexadeka, sixteen which designates a numbering system in which the bass used is 16). In MIDI communication it is common to use 7-bit Hexadecimal numbers rather than Decimal numbers. Examples only follow (not complete):

> Decimal number "0" equals Hexadecimal number "00H".
> Decimal number "1" equals Hexadecimal number "01H".
> Decimal number "2" equals Hexadecimal number "02H".
> Decimal number "10" equals Hexadecimal number "0AH".
> Decimal number "20" equals Hexadecimal number "14H".
> Decimal number "25" equals Hexadecimal number "19H".
> Decimal number "26" equals Hexadecimal number "1AH".
> Decimal number "95" equals Hexadecimal number "5FH".
> Decimal number "127" equals Hexadecimal number "7FH".

Hiatus *(Lat.)* A gap or imperfect harmony.

Hief-horn *(Ger.)* A hunting horn.

High Frequency Signal waveforms, that move at a fast rate of repetition (see *Frequency).*

His *(Ger.)* The note B sharp.

H moll *(Ger.)* Key of B minor.

Hoboe, Hoboy, Hautboy *(Ger.)* An oboe, Hoboes-plural.

Hold A character indicating that the time of a note or rest is to be prolonged *(Fermata).* ⌒

Homophony Unison; two or more voices singing in unison, the same note.

Horn See French Horn.

Hörner *(Ger.)* The horns.

Hornpipe An old English dance in a lively tempo.

Hurdy-gurdy An old instrument with four strings, which rubbed by a wheel serving as a bow. Two of the strings play the melody, while the others serve as a drone bass.

Hymn A religious or sacred song.

Hyper *(Gr.)* Above.

Hypercardioid Microphones are highly sensitive in front with less sensitivity on the sides. There would be less feedback with this unit.

Hypo *(Gr.)* Below.

I

I *(It.)* The (masculine plural.)

Idyl., Idylle *(Fr. & Ger.)*, **Idillio** *(It.)* A short poem or composition in pastoral style; an eclogue.

Il *(It.)* The.

Ilarita *(It.)* Hilarity, cheerfulness, mirth.

Il basso *(It.)* The fundamental tone; the lowest note of a chord; The bass part.

Il canto *(It.)* The song.

Il piu *(It.)* The most.

Im *(Ger.)* In the.

Imdegnato *(It.)* anger, furiously and passionately.

Imitándo *(It.)* Imitating.

Imitation, *(Lat.)* **Imitatio** *(Fr.)* **Imitation** *(It.)* **Imitazióne** *(Ger.)* **Nachahmung.** The repetition of a motive, phrase, or theme proposed by one part sometimes called the antecedent is answered by another part sometimes called the consequent. It can be an exact repetition or it can be a modification of it.

Imitation, augmented The imitation is given with notes of a greater value than those of the subject.

Imitation, diminished The imitation is given with notes of a lesser value than those of the subject.

Imitation, free Where the order of successive notes is not retained.

Immer *(Ger.)* Always, ever.

Impaziénte *(It.)* Impatient, hurried.

Imperfect fifth The diminished fifth.

Impromptu *(Fr.)* An improvisation.

Improvisation Music played without written notation. Sometime, a leadsheet may be used to show the structure of the melody and chord progression. It is music from within a performer as displayed by modern musicians playing with small groups or solo. It is a way that a musician/keyboard player will perform *what is felt within.* With the *MIDI,* the performers playing can be captured, later played back, and with the correct software, the music may be written out *(see Rap Music, Scat Singer).*

Incordaménto *(It.)* The tension of strings on a stringed instrument.

Incordáre *(It.)* To put strings on an instrument.

Indeciso *(It.)* Undecided, wavering, hesitating.

Indications scéniques *(Fr.)* Stage directions.

Indifferént, Indifferenteménte, Indifferenza *(It.)* Coldly, with indifference.

Infernále *(It.)* Infernal, diabolic.

Infervoráto *(It.)* Fervent and impassioned.

Inflammataménte *(It.)* Ardently, impetuously.

Infinito *(It.)* Perpetual.

Inflection Change or modification in the tone or pitch of the voice.

In frétta *(It.)* hastily.

Infuriánte, Infuriáto *(It.)* Furious.

Ingánno *(It.)* A deception as applied to a deceptive, an interrupted cadence, an unusual resolution of a dissonance or an unexpected modulation.

Innario *(It.)* Hymn book.

Inneggiare *(It.)* To compose or sing hymns.

In pálco *(It.)* Applies to a musical production performed on the stage.

Input Information put or transferred into a computer from an external source as a keyboard, MIDI, mouse, disk drive, modem or any peripherals that give input signals.

Input Device Any peripheral that puts data into a computer.

Input/Output Controller A form of *Interface* that controls the pathway of messages between the computer and its connected peripherals. As unlike devices may produce audio signals at different levels, including amplitudes, one may encounter problems. Certain Inputs and outputs have been designed to handle signals within certain levels as silence to a maximum value. With mismatched levels, between an apparatus, can be the cause of a problem such as a high level output being connected to a low level input, or vice versa. (Examples): A synthesizer or keyboard is connected from a line out, to a line in to a computer or mixer. A microphone, CD player (line out) is connected to a line in.

Input Peripheral refers to devices that send information to the **CPU** such as disk drives, cassette tape players, keyboards and drum pads for **MIDI** control, light pens.

Insegnaménto *(It.)* Reference to instruction.

Insensibilménte *(It.)* Little by little by small degrees.

Instrument Classification: String Percussion the Piano. String Bowing by friction *[these can also be plucked]* the Violin, Viola, Violoncello ('cello), Contrabass (Bass). String plucking the Harp, Guitar, Mandoline, Zither, Banjo, Harpischord. Wind instruments of wood, metal or man products - open mouth piece the Flute, Piccolo and Fife. Single reed would include the Clarinet and Saxophone families. Double Reeds would include the Oboe, English Horn, Bassoon and Contra Bassoon. Brass Instruments with cupped mouthpiece would include Cornet, Trumpet, French Horn, Trombone [both slide and keyed), Tuba, Sousaphone & Bugle. Instruments of percussion with various pitches would include the Kettle Drums [Tympani], Xylophone, Glockenspiel and Bells. Those without pitch would include Bass Drum, Snare Drum, Military Drum, Cymbals, Gong, Tambourine, Castagnettes and Triangle. It is interesting to note that many of the organs had/have these instruments as stops. The Digital Keyboards, Organs, Pianos, MIDI Instruments have these instruments in their Banks or storage space, or are taken from floppy disks. Mostly all are taken from true samples that prove most realistic.

Instrumental   A term which is applied to music composed or performed on instruments.

Instrumental score   A score or chart in which the instrumental parts are given in full.

Instrumentation   The make-up of various instruments to create an ensemble such as an orchestra or band.

Intavoláre *(It.)* Writing notes or copying music, a copiest.

Intavolatúra *(It.)* Musical notation and figured bass.

Intelligent Synthesizer, see MIDI SHOW CONTROL

Intelligent System of Music (ISM) created by Roland which consists of digital piano, digital sequencer with synthesizer sound modules. These usually are for educational purposes with teaching material recorded on a disk as well as entertainment. Also there are Standard MIDI Files (SMF) with printed music.

In tempo *(It.)* In time.

Intendant *(Fr.)*, **Intendénte** *(It.)* A director, conductor, impresário.

Interlude   A short piece of music usually introduced between the acts of a drama, play or musical. A short strain played between the verses of a hymn or song.

Intermezzo *(It.)* A short piece; an interlude.

Interval   The difference in pitch between two tones.

Intimissimo *(It.)* Expressive, with great feeling.

Intimo *(It.)* Inward feeling, expressive.

Intonation   The production of tone, either vocal or instrumental.

Intonato *(It.)* Tuned, set to music.

Intrepido,   **Intrepidamente** *(It.)* Intrepid, bold.

Introduction   A preliminary phrase in a composition to prepare the listener for that which follows. It may be short or long.

Invention   A short piece in free contrapuntal style.

Inversion   A change in positions referring to intervals and chords.

Ira *(It.)* Anger, wrath, passion.

Iráta, Iráto, Irataménte *(It.)* Angrily, passionately.

Irlandais *(Fr.)*, Irlandisch *(Ger.)* An air or dance tune in the Irish style.

Ironico *(It.)* Ironical.

Irregolare *(It.)* Irregular.

Irresolúto *(It.)* Irresolute, wavering.

Isdegno, con *(It.)* With indignation.

ISM, see *Intelligent System of Music.*

Ismania, con *(It.)* Wildness and madness.

Istesso *(It.)* The same.

Istrepito, con *(It.)* With noise and bluster.

Italian sixth A chord composed of a major third and an augmented sixth. (F-A-D#)

Italiano *(It.)* **Italienisch** *(Ger.)*, **Italienne** *(Fr.)* Italian.

J

Jack In the harpsichord, it is the piece of wood that contains the quill or piece of leather that serves as a plectrum plucking the strings. The *Jack* in the action of the piano causes the hammer to trip and release. A plug socket on a computer, tape recorder, microphone, and other electronic devices.

Jaeger, Jagd *(Ger.)* Hunting.

Jaléo *(Spa.)* A national Spanish dance.

Jarábe *(Spa.)* A Spanish dance.

Jeu *(Fr.)* Play, the style of playing on an instrument, A registration in an organ.

Jeu céleste *(Fr.)* The name of a soft stop in an organ formed from two dulciana pipes. The pitch of one is slightly raised giving it a waving character.

Jeux *(Fr. pl.)* Stops or registers in an organ or harmonium.

Jew's harp A small metallic instrument shaped like a lyre with a thin vibrating tongue of thin metal which is set into vibration with the forefinger.

Jig A light brisk dance.

Jingle A commercial using singing voices.

Jocosus *(Lat.)* Merry, funny and happy.

Joie *(Fr.)* Joy, gladness.

Jota *(Spa.)* A Spanish national dance usually in triple time and rapid movement.

Joueur de flûte *(Fr.)* A flutist.

Joueur musette *(Fr.)* A bagpiper.

Joueur d'instrumens *(Fr.)* A player of musical instruments.

JSMC, see *MMA.*

Jubelad *(Ger.)* Rejoicing.

Jubel-gesang, Jubel-lied *(Ger.)* Song of jubilee.

Jubilee A season of great public joy and festivity.

Jubilóso *(It.)* Jubilant & exulting.

Just A term used that applies to consonant intervals. It also applies to voices, strings and pipes that are accurate in values of time, tone, harmony, purity of intonation and execution.

Juste *(Fr.)* Correct, with regard to intonation, time and pitch.

Justo, con *(It.)* With exact precision.

K

Kammer *(Ger.)* Chamber.

Kanon *(Ger.)* A canon.

Kanzel-lied *(Ger.)* Hymn before the sermon.

Kapelle *(Ger.)* Chapel.

Kettle-drum A brass or copper shell with a skin stretched over the top. It has definite pitch and a range of a fifth or more.

Key The lever by which the sounds of a piano, organ and keyboard instruments are produced. It is the series of tones forming any given major or minor scale. The signature of a given key also serves for its relative minor key.

Keyboard The whole row of keys or levers used to produce sounds on a keyboard instrument as an acoustic piano, electronic piano, digital piano and organ. The typewriter like keys used to put information into a computer.

Keyboard Assignment Pertains to giving certain piano or keyboard keys, different functions to do. Instrumental voices can be assigned as well as various percussion sounds. If an instrument has a split keyboard, the upper portion can be assigned one set of instruments, and the lower portion a different set. If one has an organ, the lower manual (keyboard) can have one set of voices, and the upper another set. The pedal can be independent of both. With this control, and along with automatic percussion, one can introduce a full orchestra played by one user.

Keyboard Buffer A small area of storage set aside to hold the instruction of the last keystroke pressed on the keyboard. This enables the computer to accept typing commands although the computer may be busy.

Keyboard equivalents is a combination of key presses, rather than a mouse action, to perform a given function. Often these are referred to as *Command-key equivalents* or *Keyboard shortcuts.*

Keyboard Percussion Percussion sounds programmed into specific keyboard keys of organs, keyboards and MIDI instruments.

Keyboard Split Different sounds or voices may be assigned to the left and the right side of a keyboard.

Key Numbers The number of keys on a piano keyboard starting with the lowest key on the left side. The standard piano keyboard is 88 notes, although one piano company extended this in the lower and upper registers. The standard MIDI keyboard of today contains 61 keys, or five octaves. Pertaining to the MIDI key numbers, 60 is considered to be *middle C.* On the standard piano keyboard, it would be key number 40.

Keyboard Teachers Association International *(KTAI)* is a non-profit organization of Keyboard teachers throughout the world who are associated with Music Dealers, Manufacturers, all involved with the *MIDI,* its usage and functions. Their primary function is in education, evaluations, review of keyboard publications, and better keyboard teaching.

Keynote The sound or letter name in which any given scale begins. The tonic.

Kill File Delete a file.

Kit A small violin.

Kitar A musical instrument of the Arabs.

Klang *(Ger.)* Sound, tune, ringing.

Klavier *(Ger.)* A keyboard stringed instrument.

Kleine Flöte *(Ger.)* Small flute.

Kluge When one has to go through several processes to make one change and then re-enter. It is like an automobile engine, where the mechanic has to remove several parts to replace one item, and then returns all removed articles back to their original places.

Kraft *(Ger.)* Strength, vigour, energy.

Kreuz *(Ger.)* A sharp (see *Accidentals*).

KTAI (see *Keyboard Teachers Association International*).

Kurz *(Ger.)* Short.

L

L Abbreviation of the word "left,"

La The solfeggio name for the sixth degree of the scale. In France and Italy "A" is called "La."

La *(Fr. and It.)* The.

La Bemol *(Fr.)* The note A flat.

La Bemol Majeur *(Fr.)* Key of A flat major.

La Bemol Mineur *(Fr.)* Key of A flat minor.

La Majeur *(Fr.)* Key of A major.

Lamentabile *(It.)* Lamentable, mournful.

La mineur *(Fr.)* Key of A minor.

Lampons *(Fr.)* Drinking songs.

Landerer, Landler *(Ger.)* Country dance.

Largamente, Largamento *(It.)* Largely, fully, in a full free broad style of performance.

Larghetto *(It.)* Rather slow but not as slow as Largo.

Largo *(It.)* Very slow.

Lavalier Microphone A small unit worn on the lapel. Often times it is called a lapel mike.

Layering is playing two or more sounds using one piano key only.

LCD The *Liquid Crystal Display* that shows letter, numbers, images, drums, and other voices on a synthesizer. It is a technology used in flat panel display.

LD-ROM A compact disk that allows computer instruction to be recorded on a 12 inch disk as video and audio tracks (see *CD-ROM*).

Le *(Fr. and It.)* The.

Lead Refers to a solo instrument as a *Clarinet, Trumpet, Flute, Trombone, Piano, Violin, Oboe* and other instruments.

Leading-note The major seventh of any scale. The semitone below the keynote.

Lead sheet Melody line, chords and lyrics of a song are contained on manuscript paper.

Ledger, Leger lines are the short additional lines placed above or below the staff to place notes.

Legato *(It.)* Opposite to staccato. Slur, connect together.

Leger *(Fr.)* Light, nimble.

Legerete *(Fr.)* Lightness and agility.

Leggieramente, Leggiere, Leggiero, Leggiermente *(It.)* Easily, lightly, delicately.

Leise *(Ger.)* Low, soft, gentle.

Leitmotif *(Ger.)* A leading motive. A phrase or theme that is characteristic of a person or situation. Wagner used in operas.

Lentando *(It.)* With increased slowness.

Lento *(It.)* Slow.

Lesto *(It.)* Lively, nimbly, quickly.

LFO, see *Modulation*.

Libretto *(It.)* The text of an opera.

Lie *(Fr.)* Smoothly, legato.

Liebhaber *(Ger.)* A music lover.

Lieblich-gedacht *(Ger.)* An organ diapason stop of a sweet tone.

Lied *(Ger.)* A song.

Lied-buch *(Ger.)* A song book.

Ligare *(It.)* Join together; to bind, tie.

Lilt *(Scottish)* Singing or playing in a happy, jovial, merry way.

Linea *(It.)* The line of a staff.

Linke Hand *(Ger.)* The left hand.

Lip Sync   The recording of performer mouthing the words to pre-recorded track.

Liquid Crystal Display The full name for *LCD* (see *LCD*).

Liscio *(It.)* Simple, unadorned, smooth.

Litany A solemn form of pleading in worship.

Local Control   A MIDI function that will determine whether or not a Local MIDI will control from its keyboard (Local On) or by another (Local Off).

Loco *(It.)* Play as written. Used after 8va.

Log Second by second timing breakdown of a day's programming as broadcast.

Long spiel   Ancient Icelandic musical instrument played with a bow.

Looping Where a certain passage in an audio or MIDI recording is repeated as many times as desired. When used in sampling, it is commonly used to repeat a sustained section that continues to play as long as a key is held. On some keyboards it may not be necessary to hold the key(s).

Loudspeaker converts electrical signals within the range of 15 HZ to 20 kHz into audible sound. The built in loudspeaker in the computer serves as a warning device.

Lo stesso *(It.)* The same.

Loure *(Fr.)* A dance of slow time.

Lugúbre *(It.)* Sad and mournful.

Lullaby Soft gentle song.

Luth *(Fr.)* A lute.

Lunga pausa *(It.)* A long pause or rest.

Lusingando, Lusingante, Lusinghevole *(It.)* Coaxing, caressing.

Lustig *(Ger.)* Merry, gay lively.

Luttuoso *(It.)* Sorrowful, mournful.

Lyre   An ancient stringed instrument. A species of the harp.

Lyrics Words set to music. Terminology has changed in this. A song was divided by verse and chorus. Usually a verse was never performed. The chorus of today is called a "hook". It is the popular feature of a song as a headline in a newspaper. The verses give the storyline as the song develops. The bridge is a connecting portion that holds a song together.

M

M Abbreviation of mezzo, metronome, mano, main, and also used in connection with other letters.

M. M. Abbreviation for Maelzel's Metronome.

Ma *(It.)* But.

Macintosh™ **Computer** when introduced in 1984 was the first popular computer to use a graphical operating system. No longer did one have to type out a string of commands that is necessary on other computers. The operator just points at menu items or symbols by selecting the action by pointing with the mouse and then clicking. Since this period of time other computer companies followed through on this mouse and clicking feature. "Windows" is now a popular concept being used for graphics without the chain of commands. This computer can be a multitalented personality in the creation of musical roles with suitable software programs and a MIDI Interface. It can become a electronic multitrack recorder that can record, edit and playback performances using one or more synthesizers attached to it. It can become a music writer, creating its own manuscript paper (music paper). It produces a plate-like quality of music notation which saves a copiest and composer much time. In composition, one can hear immediately what was created. This is like having ones orchestra in their living room. Notes can be rearranged and changed in hundreds of different ways and SAVED for a later creation. Sound Track Production for films and recording studios use *SMPTE* which allows the engineers to synchronize a sound tract with action.

Madrigal A vocal composition of a contrapuntal nature for several voices or chorus.

Madrigále *(It.)* A Madrigal.

Madrigalésco *(It.)* Pertaining to a madrigal.

Maestevolé, **Maesta**, **Maestáde**, **Maestáte** *(It.)* Majestic, dignity, grandeur.

Maéstoso *(It.)* Majestic, stately, dignified.

Maéstro *(It.)* A master conductor, composer, artist.

Maéstro di camera *(It.)* Leader, conductor of chamber music.

Maéstro di canto *(It.)* A master of singing.

Maéstro di cappélla *(It.)* Director of musical performances in church or chapel.

Maggioláta *(It.)* A song or hymn in dedication to the month of May.

Maggiore *(It.)* The major key.

Magnetic Field is the magnetic effect in the space around a magnet. It is most important that one keeps disks away from magnets, as the disk can be erased automatically. This is true of being near a loudspeaker, or any machine that generates alternating magnetic fields which can include monitors, TV receivers and electric motors. Strong magnetic fields are generated at the tapehead and disk heads in a tape recorder and disk drives.

Main *(Fr.)* The hand.

Main droite *(Fr.)* Right hand.

Main gauche *(Fr.)* Left hand.

Maitre *(Fr.)* A master, a director.

Major Greater in respect to intervals, scales.

Major modus *(Lat.)* The major mode.

Major scale The diatonic scale having semi-tones between the third and fourth, and the seventh and eighth tones.

Malanconía, Malencónico *(It.)* Melancholy, sadness.

Mancándo *(It.)* diminishing in strength, fading away.

Mandola *(It.)* A mandoline or cithern about the size of a large lute.

Mandoline A Spanish instrument of the guitar species. It has frets like a guitar, four pairs of strings and is tuned like a violin.

Mano *(It.)* The hand.

Mano destra *(It.)* The right hand.

Mano sinistra *(It.)* The left hand.

Manual The organ keyboard.

Manual refers to the instruction book that comes with the computer or any program. It is also the name used for an Organ keyboard.

Manuscript, Manuscriptum *(La.)* Music notation written on manuscript paper consisting of 5 lines and four spaces.

Marcándo, Marcáto *(It.)* Marked, accented.

March A military piece of music to accompany marching troops usually written for brass, winds and drums.

Marcia *(It.)* A march.

Martelláto *(It.)* Hammered, strongly marked.

Martráza *(It.)* Spanish dance.

Mascharada, Mascheráta *(It.)* Music composed for grotesque characters as masquerade music.

Maschera *(It.),* **Mask, Maske** *(Ger.),* **Masque** *(Fr.)* A musical drama, operetta which includes singing and dancing performed by people wearing masks.

Massig *(Ger.)* Moderate.

Master The original copy used in any medium.

Master Volume Controls the overall volume on a synthesizer.

Mazurka *(Ger.)* A Polish dance with a lively character.

MDM see *Digital Tape Modular Digital Multitracks.*

MDR is the abbreviation for the *Music Disk Recorder.*

Measure Portion of music enclosed between two bar lines.

Mechanical Royalties refers to money a record company pays for the right to manufacture and distribute compact discs, audio cassettes, usually referred to as phonorecords, containing songs owned by a music publisher. Statutory rates were established by the 1976 Copyright Law, rates may also be negotiated.

Mediant The third degree of the scale.

Melody On Chord Transforms a single sound into a chord based upon the structure used on the lower keyboard of an electronic organ.

Metal Zone Pedal Transforms guitar tones into a new medium of raunchy, thrashy, heavy metal sounds.

Melancolie *(Fr.)* Melancholy, in a mournful style.

Melodia *(It.)* Melody, tune.

Melody A succession of tones, rhythmically arranged to produce a pleasing effect.

Meno *(It.)* Less.

Menuet *(Fr.)* Menuetto *(It.)* A minuet, a slow dance in 3/4 time.

Metronome Mechanical time beater.

Mezza, mezzo *(It.)* Medium, half.

Mezzo forte *(It.) moderately loud, indicated by* **mf.**

Mezzo piano *(It.)* softly indicated by **mp.**

Mi *(It.)* The second degree of the major scale in solfeggio. The name of the note "E" in France and Italy.

Mi bemol *(Fr.)* The note E flat.

Mi bemol majeur *(Fr.)* Key of E flat major.

Mi bemol mineur *(Fr.)* Key of E flat minor.

Microfloppy refers to a small disk as 3.5.

Microphones, see *Bidirectional Microphones, Cardioid Microphones, Condenser Microphones, Contact Pickup, Crystal or Ceramic Microphones, Dynamic Microphones, Electret Microphone, Hypercardioid Microphones, Lavalier Microphones, Omnidirectional Microphones, Ribbon or Velocity Microphone, Parabolic Microphone, Piezoelectric Microphone, Pressure-response Microphones, Shotgun Microphones.*

Middle C The note on the first ledger line below the treble staff and the first ledger line above the bass staff.

MIDI is an abbreviation for *Musical Instruments Digital Interface,* a standard means of communication with digital instruments and computer. MIDI Was Developed In 1982. MIDI Interface can become a electronic multitrack recorder that can record, edit and playback performances using one or more synthesizers attached to it. It can become a music writer, creating its own manuscript paper (music paper). It produces a plate-like quality of music notation which saves a copiest and composer much time. In composition, one can hear immediately what was created. This is like having ones orchestra in their living room. Notes can be rearranged and changed in hundreds of different ways and SAVED for a later creation. Sound Track Production for films and recording studios use *SMPTE* which allows the engineers to synchronize a sound track with action. Within its technical specifications is the desire to connect all electronic instruments and computers from various manufacturers to share information as to how the instrument is played and to integrate a music system applicable to ones needs. Layering gives the sound of two distinct instruments even though one plays one key. It allows one to play a synthesizer modules from a MIDI keyboard.

MIDI Channel A system that independently address up to 16 MIDI devices over a single MIDI cable.

MIDI CLOG A sound may be overloaded which makes gaps in notes and sounds. This can happen if the system is picking data up too slowly because of continuous controller events. The fault can be blamed on the time limitation of incoming MIDI data. A faster synthesizer can eliminate this problem or even a CPU accelerator add-on cards.

MIDI Communications does not communicate the actual sounds. It communicates performance data only as to how hard a key was struck, what note(s) are being held, additional pressure after being struck, how a key is released, information on switches, pedals, modulation, pitch blend and a patch or program number.

MIDI Connectors are *IN, OUT* and *THRU.*

MIDI Defaults Factory presets that take over when the MIDI is activated. On certain programs, applications may be set up with defaults needed each day. These would then take preference.

Mi diese *(Fr.)* The note E sharp.

Midi Disk *(MD)* A variant of a compact disk, about two and a half inches in diameter and about 4.5 inches in length. It can be programmed for input and output, meaning what is on it may be erased and be rewritten (rewritable disk as a tape).

MIDI Foot Controller A control status for the users foot. It enables the user to select programs and control many functions on a *MIDI* Instrument connected to it.

MIDI In For listening. The receiver is the *slave.*

MIDI Interface Changes data output of a computer into the information required to operate *MIDI* devices. For those of you who are not familiar with an interface, **O**pcode, **P**assport and **M**ark of the Unicorn make these for Macintosh and other computers.

MIDI Machine Control *(MMC)* Allows one to control each piece of equipment in a MIDI studio from a single source.

MIDI Manufacturers Association, see *MMA.*

MIDI OUT Sending sounds out (speaking) from an instrument to a MIDI IN connection. This is called the *master* or *instrument controller.*

MIDI Patch Bay A *Thru Box* used to connect complex setups. This is important as *MIDI* time lags are prevented when several musical instruments are connected together as in a *Daisy Chain.*

MIDI Percussion Map The key numbers, 35 to 81, on Channel #10 in relationship to Drum Sounds. Each key on the MIDI Keyboard Instrument has a different Percussion sound. Examples would include Bass Drum, Ride Cymbal, Cowbell, Woodblock, and more.

MIDI PLUGS/Jacks Connects for "In" or "Out", that is input or output. Each has five pins. Three pins are used for the purpose of MIDI and the other two connectors carry power from an AC adopter to a modified controller or another device.

MIDI Port enables a computer to be connected directly to a synthesizer.

MIDI Show Control Designed to allow MIDI systems to communicate. This works in many ways as intelligent control of various equipment used in providing commands for lights in theatres, CD players, audio tape machines, amplifiers, robots, video, film, slide projections, explosions, fog, smoke, multimedia plus many other aspects. Roland Musical Instruments also has their intelligent instrument called, Intelligent Synthesizer, E series.

MIDI Time Code A synchronization signal that allows MIDI based equipment to follow absolute timing reference which is independent of tempo (see *SMPTE, SMPTE CODE*).

MIDI Time Lag - When a number of *MIDI* devices are connected to a single output, there could be a delay in response time.

MIDI TIMING CLOCKS Specifies certain number of measures, beats, what beat of the measure the composition starts on. It also relates to SMPTE Time Codes (see *Anacrusis*).

MIDI THRU is similar to **MIDI Out** as it does not speak to the next instrument. It does not supply its own conversation, but repeats anything heard by MIDI In. As this information is not addressed to anything specific, it can be passed on to other devices as being *daisy-chained* with all responding to a MIDI controller, keyboard, computer or any other implement capable of producing MIDI data.

Mignon *(Fr.)* Dainty, charming.

Mike A term used for the word *microphone.*

Mi majeur *(Fr.)* Key of E major.

Mi mineur *(Fr.)* Key of E minor.

Minacciando, Minaccievole *(It.)* Threatening, menacing.

Ministudio A portable self-contained recording studio. Musical ideals can be worked out any place. It is possible to work out a four or eight track format by bouncing tracks. These tape decks have different tape speeds, pitch control, noise reduction, frequency response, punch in, and looping.

Minor Less; smaller; in speaking of intervals.

Minor diatonic scale There are three forms of this scale. In the Natural, Pure or Historic form, the notes are from the Relative Major Scale. The Harmonic form has the semi-tones between the second and third, and seventh and eighth degrees, both in ascending and descending. Between the sixth and seventh scale degrees, it has the interval of an augmented second. In the Melodic form the semi-tones are between the second and third, and seventh and eighth degrees in ascending. In descending it takes the Natural form.

Minuet, see *Menuet.*

Missa brevis *(Lat.)* A short Mass.

Misteriosamente, Misterioso *(It.)* Mysterious.

Mit *(Ger.)* With, by.

Mix The technique of combining different audio tracks.

Mixer Part of a sound system that mixes sounds.

MMA The MIDI Manufacturers Association and the Japanese MIDI Standards Committee (JSMC). These would be the MIDI caretakers which have adopted Continuous Controller messages as Standard MIDI Files (SMFs), MIDI Time Code (MTC) and Sample Dump Files (SDS). General MIDI (GS) was developed about 1991, Show Control in 1993 and MIDI Machine Control (MMC) in 1992.

MMC, see *MMA,* and *MIDI Machine Control.*

Mobile *(It.)* *Moveable, changeable.*

Modal transposition, see *Transposition.*

Mode A species of scale. In the present system of music there are only two modes, the major and minor. In the ancient Greek and the mediaeval ecclesiastical system there were many more.

Mode designates the different functions of a keyboard as *play mode* and *record mode.* It is a method of operation.

Moderato *(It.)* Moderately; in moderate time.

Modesto *(It.)* Modestly, quietly, moderately.

Modulation In music, it would be a transition part leading from one key into another key. When applied to the voice, it means to change the tone to a certain degree of intensity, or light and shade.

Modulation used with MIDI, it is the modification of some of the characteristics of a wave form. The effects can take place when the parameters are varied, either automatically or manually. For automatic modulation, a low frequency oscillator *(LFO)* or the envelope generator *(EG)* is used to control the value(s) of the selected parameter. Manually, one can use a foot pedal or MIDI controller (See *Flanger, Choruses, Pitch Shifting,* and *Phase Shifting).*

Modulation Wheels Include, lead pan, lead slide, known as portamento and the wah-wah.

Modulator A miniature transmitter.

Modules Expanders (add ons to be joined) to the users original system as extra sounds and keyboards. If one has a Keyboard, a stand for the keyboard could be added, or a pedalboard, or a bench to sit on, among other attachments. This would also refer to Integrated Software as well.

Moins *(Fr.)* Less.

Moll *(Ger.)* Minor.

Molle *(Fr.)* Soft, mellow, delicate.

Mollemente (It.) Softly, gently, delicately.

Mollis *(Lat.)* Soft.

Molta *(It.)* **Molto** *(It.)*: Much, very much; extremely.

Mono   One.

Monocorde *(Fr.)* **Monocordo** *(It.)* On one string only.

Monophonic When only one sound can be played at a time. It simulates acoustic instruments as well as solo lines where the user only requires a single note (see *Mono).*

Monotone refers to one and the same sound.

Mono Voices would be one solo or a lead voice as a vocalist, violin, clarinet, trombone, in opposition to *Poly Voices.*

Mordante *(It.)* See *Mordent.*

Mordent *(It.)* The mordent consists of three notes — the principal, lower auxiliary, and principal. The inverted mordent contains the principal, upper auxiliary, and the principal. The first two notes are played quickly and the third is held longer. Accidentals may be used.

Morendo *(It.)* Gradually diminishing the tone.

Mosso *(It.)* Movement, motion.

Motet, Motett, Motette *(Ger.)* **Motet** *(Fr.)* **Motetto** *(It.)* A sacred composition for several voices.

Motif *(Fr.)* A motive, or figure.

Motion   The movement of a melody or part.

Motion, Contrary   The movement of one part moving in an opposite direction of another part.

Motion, Direct   Movement of two or more parts in the same direction.

Motion, oblique   One part remains stationary while   another part ascends or descends.

Moto *(It.)* Motion, movement.

Motus *(Lat.)* Movement.

Mouse   Small handheld device which one moves around on a flat surface in order to position the cursor on a video or computer display.

MOS   *Mit Out Sound,* a silent shoot or take.

MSC, see *MIDI Show Control.*

MTC, see *MMA.*

Multi Presets ROM/ROM Referring to Multitimbral sound   modules where several single presets, each on a specific MIDI channel can be saved as Multitimbral.

Multichannel Audio Digital Interface *(MADI)* A professional standard for transmitting up to 56 channels   of digital audio data over a single cable.

Multimedia may be an integration of various aspects dealing with the workings of computers. This takes into effect combinations of animation, graphics music, speech, text, video and even live performance. Usually all of this is computer controlled that is sent out by the airwaves and enters your television screen for viewing.

Multitimbral, multitimbrality The ability of a synthesizer or vibration sound module to sound more than one voice at a time on each key when going through different MIDI channels simultaneously. This is useful when creating a full orchestra or ensemble. An electronic instrument may contain 192 or more sounds referred to as patches. The reasoning for this is in going back to early electronic instruments. Electronic cables were used called patch cords for reconfiguring their timbre. Other terms used in reference to patches would be *preset, program setup* and *instrument* even using the word *voice* rather than *patch*. Each sound or timbral may be assigned to a separate *MIDI* Channel (see *FM, FM-Poly Voices*).

Multitimbral Sequencing Playing more than one instrument or sound at a time.

Multitimbral Sound Module An inexpensive way to expand the sounds of the Digital Piano.

Multitrack recording Consists of two or more separate tracks which may be edited, as to volume, to fit in with all other tracks. Track One may be violins: Track Two may be basses; Track Three may be piano: Track Four may be percussion.

Multiple Tracking Singers re-recording over original track or adding additional track(s) containing the same material (same notes) as recorded on original track.

Movement A division, or part of an extended composition.

Musetta *(It.)* **Musette** *(Fr.)* A small bagpipe; a primitive oboe. A composition, or movement of a composition with a drone-bass.

Musica *(It.)* Music.

Music Notation Program Software for a computer that displays notation on the screen or monitor. It can be edited and printed as sheet music. It may be entered by MIDI instrument, or by a mouse.

Musical Instruments Digital Interface *(MIDI)* A synthesizer-communications standard put into practically every synthesizer made.

Music Disk Recorder *(MDR)* A digital recorder using a floppy disk (3.5) as a recording medium. It also has editing functions as *Punch In Recording, Remote Control of Playback, Repeated Playback and Volume*, and *Tempo Adjustment (see Disk Drive)*.

Music Sequencer (see *Sequencer*).

Musicstation may consist of a computer, interface and a keyboard. These are usually used in a school system, on a desk type platform with wheels that can be moved from classroom to classroom easily. On professional level, much more would be added to this according to the production company's needs.

Music Styles usually refers to styles of Rock, Jazz, Big Band, Waltzes, Mazurkas, Blue Grass, Twist, Shuffle, Blues, Bossa Nova, Latin and many more including Users styles.

Musique-Concrete was one of the first important breakthroughs in electronic music when all the music was made by manipulating prerecorded sounds.

Myoelectric (see *COSMETIC GLOVE*).

Musa *(Lat.)* A song.

Musique *(Fr.)* Music.

Mute A way of silencing some instrumental tracks when a mixing session is going on. A small object of wood, metal or ivory placed on the bridge of a string instrument to dampen the tone. In a brass instrument an object is placed in the bell to modify the tone.

Muthig *(Ger.)* Courageous, spirited.

Mystères *(Fr.)* Mysteries Sacred drama with music. The predecessors of the oratorio.

N

Naif *(Fr.)* Naiv *(Ger.)* Naive *(Fr.)* Simple, natural.

NAMM The abbreviation for the *National Association of Music Merchants* who have encouraged the *MIDI* all the way.

Narrante *(It.)* In a narrative style.

Natural A character used to cancel a sharp or flat (see *Accidentals*).

Neapolitan sixth A chord constructed of a root, a minor third and a minor sixth occurring on the fourth degree of the scale. Example: Key of C; F-Ab-Db.

Needle Drop Using prerecorded music rather than new music composed for a commercial.

Negligente *(It.)* Negligent, unconstrained.

Network A connecting system which allows simultaneous broadcast or telecast of a single program or commercial by a number of stations.

Netto *(It.)* Neat, quick, clear, nimble.

Neu *(Ger.)* New.

Nicht *(Ger.)* Not.

Ninth An interval consisting of an octave and a second.

Nobile *(It.)* Noble, grand, impressive.

Nocturne *(Fr.)* A night piece of romantic character.

Noel *(Fr.)* A Christmas carol, or hymn.

Noise A signal that contains an even distribution of possible frequency within a certain range. These are described as colors, white, pink, red, green, blue and azure. This *noise* can produce a richness to the sounds. Noise on a recording may be mechanical caused by long cables. A SCSI cable longer than six feet may cause a problem. Make sure it is a double-shielded cable. A noisy computer fan could also be the culprit. An analogue hiss could even be caused by a sound card. This also applies to **VCA** (see *Compresser, Ducking, Gates, VCA)*.

Non *(It.)* Not, no.

Nona *(It.)* Interval of a ninth.

Non-Real Time Music Composing, or creating a piece step by step by a computer. This can be entered in by a computer keyboard, a mouse, or a real musical instrument keyboard. Also one can have instant playback, if the computer has sound features, or is connected to a keyboard with a MIDI interface.

Nonstandard Key Signatures Getting away from the usual key signatures that we are all familiar with. Experiments dealing with sound waves, bring us away from our traditional heritage. Our major and minor scales, of twelve half steps, and   our cycle of fifths in relationship to the fifteen key signatures are becoming antiquated. If one takes a nonlinear key signature, which has no bearing to any other distribution of related key signatures, there are numerous possibilities one can relate too. In relationship to this, compare what has been done with the spectrum colors of the rainbow - red, orange, yellow, green, blue, indigo and violet in art work. In dealing with these vibrations of color, one can deal with vibrations of sound waves in various pitches. It does sound strange at first, but one grows into it. We all accept J.S. Bach today as normal listening. However in his day he was way ahead of his time. He did lose one church position because of his modernistic creative playing.

Non troppó *(It.)* Not too much, moderate.

Non troppó allégro *(It.)* Not too quick

Nota *(Lat. and It.)* A note.

Nota buona *(It.)* An accented note.

Nota cambiata *(It.)* A changing note.

Nota caratteristica *(It.)* The leading tone. In the scale of "C", C-D-E-F-G-A-B-C, it would be "B" the seventh degree of the scale. This would apply to other scales as well.

Nota cattiva *(It.)* An unaccented note.

Nota contra notam *(Lat.)* Note against note as used in Counterpoint.

Nota d'abbellimento *(It.)* A grace note.

Nota di passaggio *(It.)* A passing note.

Nota falsa *(It.)* A changing note.

Nota principale *(It.)* A principal or essential note.

Nota romana *(Lat.)* Early notation by means of points, commas and hooks. Also referred to as *melodic phrases* at the close of a verse.

Nota sensibile *(It.)* Note sensible *(Fr.)* refers to the leading note.

Nota sostenuta *(It.)* A sustained note.

Notation   Representing tones by written or printed characters. In a musical sense, means the written notes on a staff system of five lines and four spaces. See *Music Notation Program.*

Note   A sign or character that is placed in certain positions on the staff to show a certain pitch of sound. It also shows the duration of any sound by its form.

Notturno *(It.)* A nocturne; a serenade.

Nuances *(Fr.)* Shades of expression; variety of intonation.

Nuovo, nuova *(It.)* New.

Nuptial songs   Wedding, marriage songs.

Nut   The small bridge at the upper end of the fingerboard of a guitar or violin, on which the strings pass to the pegs or screws.

O

O   Triple or perfect time in medieval music. The imperfect or common time was represented by a broken circle as a "C". The sign "o" placed over a note for a string instrument indicates an open string or harmonic. *(It. - before a consonant)* Or; as; either.

OASYS *Open Architecture Synthesis System.* A system brought out by Korg. An electronic tone generation capable of performing 220 million instructions per second in the way sound is made.

Obbligato *(It.)* Obbligati *(It. plural)* Oblige *(Fr.)* Obligat *(Ger.)* An additional, or necessary part added to a composition to enhance. **Ober** *(Ger.)* Upper, higher.

Oblique motion.   When one part ascends or descends while the others remain stationary.

Oboe *(It.)* A wind instrument with a double reed *(hautboy).*

Octave   An interval of eight diatonic sounds or degrees, a span of 8. On a music keyboard, it would be C to C, eight notes higher or lower, or E to E, eight notes higher or lower. Diatonically the notes within this octave, from C to C would be C-D-E-F-G-A-B-C. The note characters used in Western Music consist of the first seven letters in the alphabet and then continue to repeat though out the spectrum of notes or sounds that may be heard.

Octavo   Folding a sheet of paper into eight leaves. This is a term used for printed *Octavo* music, usually printed for a chorus.

Octet, Octett   A composition for eight parts.

Od *(It. - before a vowel)* Or; as; either.

Ode *(Gr.)* Air or song.

Ohm   A unit of measurement pertaining to resistance.

Omnidirectional Microphone Takes in sound, equally, from all directions.

Ohne *(Ger.)* Without.

Opcode *(Operation Code)* is a word that specifies some kind of action. It can be loading, as in the use of an interface, which is a definite action between a *MIDI* and a computer.

Opens Musical introductions that cue a video production, or section.

Opera *(It.)* A drama set to music for voices and orchestra, with scenery and action.

Operetta A little opera usually in a light and playful vein.

Opus *(Lat. and Ger.)* Work, composition; used by composers to number their compositions or publications.

Orange Book, see *CD-DA*.

Oratorio *(It.)* A composition made of solos and concerted pieces for voices. The theme is taken from the Bible or sacred history.

Orchestra The part of a theatre or concert-room where the musicians play. This term also applies to the performers. The main portion of an orchestra is the string family, combined with the wood winds, brass and percussion.

Orchestration The art of composing or arranging music for orchestra; also a set of printed or written parts for orchestra.

Orchestral Voices Creates the sounds of the major sections in an orchestra, as Strings (first and second violins, violas, cellos and double basses), Brass (trumpets, trombones, French horns, bass trombone and possibly a tuba), Woodwinds (flutes, oboes, clarinets, bassoons, piccolo, English horn, bass clarinet, contrabassoon, and saxophones and Percussion (timpani, bass drum, cymbals, snare drum, and triangle). Added to this, one may find a harp, piano, celeste, wood blocks, temple blocks, whips or slapsticks, sleigh bells, xylophone, marimba, vibraphone, glockenspiel, chimes, harpsichord and organ.

Organ A keyboard (manual) instrument with pipes of different sizes made to sound by means of compressed air from bellows. Organs being made today are electronic and small enough to be used in a home, Organs have one to five manuals.

Organ-point A sustained note in one of the parts with harmonic progressions in the others. Also known as *Pedal-point*.

Organum An organ. A constant succession of fourths and fifths as used in ancient music.

Ornaments All embellishments such as *Grace notes*.

Oscillator A component that produces waves. An analog oscillator produces electrical waves and a digital oscillator produces numbers that represents waves.

Ossia *(It.)* **Or**; otherwise; or else. Indicates another way to play a passage.

Ostinato *(It.)* Continuous use of some melodic figure or group of notes.

Ottava *(It.)* An octave; an eighth.

Output, see **Input/Output Controller**.

Output Peripheral Devices as disk drives, printers, sound and voice generators that receive information from the computer for the user to make use of.

Overdub, Overdubbing is the practice of adding additional sounds, generally musical notes, to a sound track. In practice, one would listen to a track(s) and record new material on an unused track. If a mistake is made by a musician or vocalist, it can be corrected at their leisure by re-recording on the same track or a different one. The process of overdubbing can be repeated to add additional parts as their are remaining tracks. If one runs out of tracks, one can mix several tracks on one track. This is called "bouncing." Before this submix, make sure this is the sound desired. Once done, the new track cannot be changed as the original tracks no longer exist.

Overtones, see *Harmonic Series and Sounds.*

Overture An introductory part of an opera, oratorio, musical play. It may also be an independent composition.

P

P Abbreviation of Pedal (P. or Ped.); piano *(p)*, pianissimo *(pp)*, pianississimo *(ppp)*.

Pandean pipes, Pan's pipes One of the most ancient and simple musical instruments. It was made of hollow reeds or tubes of different lengths fastened together and tuned to each other. It was closed at the bottom and blown into at the top.

Panning would be a location of sound as to the left, the center or to the right speakers which are producing the sound.

Pantomime An entertainment in which no words are sung or spoken. It is expressed by action accompanied by music.

Parabolic Microphones A broadcast duty microphone which is a conventional microphone. It is linked to a reflecting surface that focuses sound on a microphone element. Because of the sensitivity and directional characteristics, it makes a great microphone to have on a set, especially at sporting events.

Parallel Intervals Consecutive intervals in the same direction .

Parallel motion The movement of two or more parts in the same direction with the same distance from each other.

Parameter can be defined as several variable parts in relationship to spaces, decimal places, rests, grace notes, sizes of notes the stems, beam depth, in *fixed* areas in various areas in relationship to music.

These are different aspects that can be controlled by the user. One can use a *Parameter* with a certain value for some time and then the value may be changed. If one does not wish to change any definitions, the program will use a default value set by the manufacturer, or the user.

Paraphrase A transcription or arrangement of a vocal or instrumental piece for another medium with variations.

Parlando, Parlante *(It.)* In a recitative or speaking style.

Partita *(It.)* An early form of the instrumental suite.

Partition *(Fr.)* **Partitur** *(Ger.)* **Partitura and Partizione** *(It.)* A full score.

Pas *(Fr.)* A step or a dance .

Passacaglia *(It.)* An old dance in triple time, usually written on a ground bass.

Passage A musical phrase; short portion of an air; a run or an arpeggio, or any part of a strain, or movement is a passage.

Passepied *(Fr.)* A lively old French dance.

Passing notes Notes which do not belong to the harmony.

Passionato *(It.)* Passionate; impassioned; with fevor and pathos.

Passione *(It.)* Passion, reeling.

Pas soul *(Fr.)* A dance by one performer.

Pastoral Pertaining to rural life.

Patch An interconnection of various parameters that activate, define or the modification of a synthesizer voice. It is a temporary modification to the software. It also refers to the connecting video and audio equipment with cables or through a central panel (see *Multitimbral)*.

Patch Bay Central routing control for signals as audio and MIDI data. At one time they used to be short cables but now they handle and store signals electronically.

Patchboard (see *Plugboard)*.

Patch Editor Software that allows the user to edit or redefine a voice, or voices of a sound module using the computer.

Pattern A set of music examples for a specified number of measures. Once it is there it can be repeated when needed. It can be transferred by the commands by *Copy* and *Paste*. If it is to be removed completely use the commands *Cut, Copy* and *Paste*. Experiment with it, to be sure, before pressing *Command and Save*.

Pauken *(Ger.)* Kettledrums.

Pausa *(It., Spa., and Lat.)* A pause.

Pavan *(Eng.)* **Pavana** *(It.)* **Pavane** *(Fr.)* A grave stately dance which took its name from *pavano,* a peacock.

Paventáto, Paventóso *(It.)* Fearful, anxiety, embarrassment.

Pedal Any mechanism controlled by the foot.

Pedal point A sustained bass or pedal note held for several measures while a variety of chords are played. Also called *Organ Point.*

Pentatonic scale A scale of five notes formed on the sounds of A-C-D-E-G. The fourth and seventh degrees are omitted. It is a primitive scale used much by the Chinese. The Scottish people have used this scale in many of their melodies. A more modern version was developed by adding the *fourth* degree, still leaving out the *seventh* degree.

Per *(It.)* For, by, from, in, through.

Percussion *(Eng.),* **Percussione** *(It.)* A general name for instruments that are struck (*Ex: drums, bells*).

Perdéndo *(It.)* **Perdendósi** *(It.)* Gradually decreasing the tone and time; dying away, becoming extinct.

Perfect A term applied to 4ths, 5ths and Octave intervals.

Perfect 4th   Perfect 5th   Perfect Octave

Performance Royalties are administered by performing-rights societies as ASCAP, BMI, and SESAC. Each country have their own societies that may work with the above three in togetherness and distributions. These are the funds songs earn when performed in public on radio and television stations, night clubs, restaurants and other venues as trade shows, parks. Revenues are distributed to writers and publishers according to the frequency of performance. As one can realize this is a gigantic task in keeping records which cannot always be accurate.

Period *(Eng.)* Periode *(Fr. and It.)* A complete and perfect musical sentence.

Pesante *(It.)* Impressive; with weight and importance.

Petit *(Fr.)* Little, small.

Petto *(It.)* The chest, the breast.

Peu *(Fr.)* Little.

Phase Two identical wave forms beginning at slightly different times. One may be high and the other low (see *Modulation*).

Phono Plug connects audio devices to a tape recorder, radio, even to the new computers that accept sound. Also called an *RCA* plug.

Phrase Part of a musical sentence; a musical thought or idea.

Phrasing Dividing the musical sentence into rhythmical sections, usually by means of a slur. The punctuation of music.

Piacere *(It.)* Pleasure. A piacere. At pleasure.

Piacevole *(It.)* Pleasing, graceful, agreeable.

Piangendo *(It.)* Wailing, lamenting, weeping.

Pianissimo *(It.)* Extremely soft (Abbrev. is *pp).*

Piano *(It.)* Soft (Abbrev. is **p**).

Pianoforte *(It.)* A well known string instrument of percussion known as the *Piano*. The tones are produced by felt covered hammers striking the strings. An instrument capable of being played soft or loud.

Piccolo *(It.)* Small, little. A small flute with a high pitched sound.

Piéna, Piéno *(It.)* Full.

Pieta, Pietosaménte, Pietóso *(It.)* Tenderly, slow and sustained.

Piezoelectric Microphone has a flexible diaphragm with a crystal element. The pressure of sound distorts the crystal into generating a corresponding voltage. It is sometimes called a **C**rystal or **C**eramic microphone.

Pipe Any tube of metal, plastic, reed or wood, which when blown into, produces a musical sound.

Pitch The rate of vibrations. Rapid vibrations mean a high tone, slow vibrations a low deep tone.

Pitch Shift is when two sounds (signals) go in and out of tune with each other (see *Modulation*).

Più *(It.)* More.

Più allégro *(It.)* A little faster, more lively.

Più fórte *(It.)* Louder.

Più lénto *(It.)* More slowly.

Più mósso, Piu moto *(It.)* More motion, quicker.

Più móto *(It.)* More motion, quicker.

Più piáno *(It.)* Piano, softer **p.**

Più Più *(It.)* Some what more.

Più présto *(It.)* Quicker, more rapid.

Più vivo *(It.)* More lively, more animated.

Pizzicáto, Pizzicándo *(It.)* Pinched, snapped or plucked.

Placenteraménte *(It.)* Joyfully.

Placidaménte *(It.)* Calmly, placidly, quietly.

Plagal cadence Final tonic chord preceded by the subdominant.

Plain chant *(Fr.)* Plain-song. The name given to the old ecclesiastical chant in its most simple state without harmony.

Playing Mode Controls refer to the accompaniment to be played as to a *one finger chord,* or *full hand chord.*

Plaque *(Fr.)* Struck at once.

Platter is used for disks. It was a common expression for the old 78 RPM Victrola records (some were 12 inches wide), as well as the $33^1/3$ and 45 RPM longer playing records. This term can now be applied to a *Compact Disk.*

Platti *(It.)* Cymbals.

Poco *(It.)* Little.

Poco a poco *(It.)* Little by little.

Poi *(It.)* Then, after, afterwards.

Poi a poi *(It.)* By degrees.

Pói ségue, Pói seguénte *(It.)* Then follows, here follows.

Polacca *(It.)* Polish dance in triple time.

Polka A lively Bohemian dance in duple time.

Polka mazurka A dance in triple time, played slowly and having the accent on the last beat of the measure.

Polka redowa A dance song in triple time, played faster than the *Polka mazurka* with the accent on the first beat.

Polonaise A Polish dance in triple rhythm.

Polyphonic Several voices; counterpoint in several parts. As used in electronic musical instruments, it refers to the ability of playing several notes at one time.

Poly Voices A combination of several voices played together, as in an orchestra, a Brass section, a Violin section, Percussion voices. *(Opposite of this would be Mono, meaning one voice.)*

Pomposo *(It.)* Pompous, stately, grand.

Ponticello *(It.)* The bridge of a violin, guitar.

Port A socket on the back of a computer, to plug in a peripheral device as a *MIDI,* another computer, printer, network.

Portable Keyboards and Pianos Electronic keyboards of various sizes. The small ones are usually battery contained.

Portamento *(It.)* A smooth gliding of a tone into another. This is the legato way of playing an instrument.

Portato *(It.)* Sustained; drawn out.

Posaune *(Ger.)* A trombone; also an organ stop.

Post A word used for *Post-Production.*

Post-production Takes place after shooting a movie. Pertains to the editing, audio sweetening and adding special effects and graphics.

Ppqn is a measurement of time resolution in sequencers in various tempi, in this case being *Pulses per Quarter Note.*

Prall-triller *(Ger.)* Inverted mordent.

Precipitato *(It.)* Hurriedly.

Preciso *(It.)* Precise, exactly.

Prelude A musical introduction played before the real performance of a composition, Opera, Drama. It also applies to other musical compositions which are on their own as the Chopin Preludes. Originally preludes consisted of a few preparatory chords.

Preludio *(Spa)* **Preludium** *(Lat.)* **Preludio** *(It.)* A prelude, or introduction.

Premier, premiere *(Fr.)* First.

Pre-roll Rewinding of tape in editing a *VCR* to a cue point. This would imply the tape is up to speed when rolled forward to the editing point.

Pre-scoring The techniques of recording music prior to shooting video portions.

Presets Voices that can be played on a keyboard without programming (see *default*).

Preset Sounds are the sounds put in a keyboard instrument by the manufacturer.

Pressante *(Fr.)* Pressing on; hurrying.

Pressure-response Microphones Couples a microphone element to a plate that can be mounted to various places as a wall, ceiling or other substantial places.

Prestézza *(It.)* Quickness, rapidity.

Prestissimaménte, Prestissimo *(It.)* Very quickly, as fast as possible.

Présto *(It.)* Quickly, rapidly.

Présto, ma non tróppo *(It.)* Quick, but slightly less.

Priére *(Fr.)* A prayer.

Prima *(It.)* First, chief, principal.

Prima donna *(It.)* Leading female singer in opera.

Prime *(Ger.)* First note, or tone of a scale.

Primo *(It.)* Principal, first.

Prímo búffo *(It.)* First male singer in a comic opera.

Prímo tenore, Prímo uómo *(It.)* First tenor singer.

Print Royalties pertain to money earned from sales of printed material.

Procella *(It.)* A storm.

Program Change refers to a MIDI command that tells the MIDI device to change to another setting.

Program music Instrumental music giving a description of objects, nature or events.

Progression Melodic progression is going from one tone to another. Harmonic progression is going from one chord to another.

Prologhétto *(It.)* A short prologue.

Pronto *(It.)* Ready, quick.

Pronunziáre *(It.)* To pronounce, to enunciate clearly.

Protagonista *(It.)* Principal character in a drama or opera.

Prothalamion *(Gr.)* A nuptial song.

Próva *(It.)* A rehearsal.

Psalm A sacred song or hymn.

Psalter A book of Psalms.

Pulse Code Modulation A process of digital recording used in CD's, samplers and video recorders.

Punch-In/Punch-Out To replace notes or certain sections of a track, rather than redoing the entire track over again.

Punctus *(Lat.),* **Punkt** *(Ger.),* **Punta** *(It.)* A dot, a point.

Puntato *(It.)* Pointed, detached, marked.

Pupitre *(Fr.)* A music desk.

Q

Quadrat *(Ger.)* **Quádro** *(It.)* The Natural sign (see **A**ccidentals).

Quadrille *(Fr.)* A French dance, or a set of five consecutive dance movements. Generally it is in 2/4 or 6/8 rhythm.

Quadruple counterpoint. Counterpoint in four parts, all of which may be inverted.

Quantization, Quantize are the names used with **Midi's** in rounding off notes to the closest rhythmic time values when played to create a readable transcription on the monitor or printed copy. This is in reference to real time transcriptions as played by the performer (see *Compression*).

Quárta, Quárto *(It.)* A fourth.

Quarter note A crotchet. A note one-fourth the value of a whole note.

Quarter (Crotchet) Note & Rest

Quarter Note Triplets

Quarter note Triplets (see *Tuplets*). Three notes played in the time of two notes.

Quarter rest A pause equal in duration to a quarter note.

Quarter tone A small interval, or deviation of pitch which is found to exist between C# and Db, F# and Gb, *etc.*

Quartet A composition for either four voices or instruments.

Quasi *(It.)* In the manner or style of, or somewhat.

Quaver *(Eng.)* An eighth-note.

Quaver (Eighth Note) & Rest

Quer-pfeife *(Ger.)* A fife.

Questa, Questo *(It.)* This or that.

Queue *(Fr.)* Tail or stem of note, tailpiece of violin.

Quieto *(It.)* Quiet, calm, serene.

Quint *(Lat.)* Quinta *(It.)* Quinte *(Fr. and Ger.)* A fifth. Also the name of an organ stop sounding a fifth or a twelfth above the foundation stops.

Quintet A composition for either five voices or instruments.

Quintole *(Lat.)*, **Quintolet** *(Fr.)* **Quintuplets** A group of five notes having the same value as four notes of the same species (see *Tuplets*).

Quintuplets

Quint-saite *(Ger.)* Treble string.

Quire A choir, a body of singers.

Quodlibet *(Lat.)* A melody of different songs as a musical potpourri.

R

R Abbreviation for "Right."

Rabbia *(It.)* Rage, fury, madness.

Raddolcendo *(It.)* With increasing softness.

Rallentamento, Rallentando, Rallentato *(It.)* The time movement goes gradually slower (Abb. *Rall*).

RAM *Random Access Memory,* Internal computer memory for programs and data that may be altered. Information in RAM will be lost if not saved before computer is turned off *(see Sound Module).*

RAP Music is not always a correct kind of music as a traditional trained musician may view it. Music may be played, but not always in the same key. It may start out as a bass line or drum rhythmical pattern. Chords later added to it with a background of voices or synthesizers. Then a lyrical pattern relating to protest, current days functions and happenings, the realism of the day are sung Intellectually, it may and should raise the social and educational consciousness to a higher level (see *Improvisation, Scat Singer).*

Rapidamente, Rapidita, Rapido *(It.)* Rapidly.

Rasch *(Ger.)* Swift, spirited.

Rattenendo, Rattenuto *(It.)* Holding back.

Rauco *(It.)* Hoarse, harsh.

RCM *Realtime Convolution & Modulation* that brings a new depth of sample realism which includes the expressive power of *FM.*

Re A syllable applied to the second degree of the scale. In Italy and France *'D'* is called *Re.*

Real-time Actually playing on a keyboard and programming it directly into a sequencer. In reference to a computer, it is the definite time it takes events to occur in a computer program. That action then goes on to a computer screen that corresponds to a *one to one ratio* in relationship to *real* clock time.

Realtime Convolution & Modulation, see *RCM.*

Re bemol *(Fr.) The note D flat.*

Re bemol majeur *(Fr.)* Key of D flat major.

Recht *(Ger.)* Right.

Recitando, Ricitante *(It.)* Declamatory, in the style of a recitative.

Recitative Declamatory singing, free in rhythm and tempo. Usually this is done with a keyboard or orchestra sounding chords only.

Recorder A device that will make a permanent, a temporary record of a signal, or a program, either being audio or video. Many keyboards and organs have their own built-in-recorders.

Redowa, Redowak, Redowazka A Bohemian dance in duple and triple time, alternately (see *Polka Redowa).*

Reed A reed, used on certain woodwind musical instruments produces the sound. It may be a thin strip of wood, cane, plastic or metal against which a current of air is directed.

Reel A lively dance from both Scotland and Ireland.

Refrain The chorus sung or played after the verse or stanza of a song or ballad.

Register The several parts of the compass of the human voice and wind instruments marked by their distinctive timbres. The stops, or set of pipes used in an organ.

Registering or Registration The proper management of the stops or drawbars in an organ.

Registration Memory A memory bank to store a favorite sound or song which can be brought forth immediately. This would also include many effects as well.

Rehearsal Practice before a given performance.

Rein (Ger.) Pure, clear, perfect.

Reiselied (Ger.) A traveling song.

Reissued Recordings There are thousands of tapes, acetate disks, metal parts or stampers from which a record was pressed in making the 78-rpm records, the 45's and the 33's which contain much music. On these, it was found much of the quality has gone. With the new technology of the CD (Compact Disk), it was found these could be reproduced with a profit realized on a 5,000 print sale. On these reissues, the producers try to find the first-generation master record or tape. These old masters are run through a computerized noise reduction system. It was found that the oxide, on the tape, containing music, could be stripped by playing the tape. However experiments found that by baking tapes, at 130 degrees, in a convection oven for eight hours, would bind the oxide. However a tape can only be cooked twice, before destruction. Once it has been decided to reissue a work, the master must be found in the archives, which contained the original 78's, or the reels of mono, stero and multitrack tapes. These tapes are then remastered into digital form to produce a CD. The extraneous noise is removed through computer process, which could also remove part of the music information. Research is then made for *liner* notes as to the original recording date, and the names of the members of the orchestra, or vocal group that performed.

Related A term applied to chords, modes or keys which admit an easy and natural transition from one to the other.

Relative keys Keys which may differ by one sharp or flat or which have the same key signature.

Religiosament, Religioso (It.) Religiously; solemnly; in a devout manner.

Re majeur *(Fr.)* D major.

Re mineur *(Fr.)* D minor.

Remote keys Keys whose scales have few tones in common, as the key of G and F sharp.

Rentree *(Fr.)* Return.

Renvoi *(Fr.)* A repeat.

Repeat A character indicating that certain measures or passages are to be sung, or played twice. These signs usually are dots preceding and following a double bar.

Repeat 8va Repeat an octave higher.

Repercussion A frequent repetition of the same sound.

Repertoire *(Fr.)* Those pieces which can be readily performed by a group or solo performer.

Repeter *(Fr.)* To repeat.

Repetimento, Repetizione *(It.)* Repetition.

Repros *(Fr.)* A pause.

Reprise *(Fr.)* A repetition or return to some previous part.

Requiem *(Lat.)* A Mass, or musical service for the dead.

Reset To return a Song at the beginning.

Reset All Controllers A MIDI message that returns all values to default or zero.

Resonance Sound, reverberation, echo.

Respiro (It.) Taking breath in singing.

Rest A character indicating silence.

Retro (Lat.) Backward; the melody reversed, note for note.

Retrograde Going backward. Playing a music melodic line in reverse.

Retto *(It.)* Right, straight, direct.

Reveille *(Fr.)* Awakening, Military, horn-music or a morning signal.

Reverberation The tones linger on, from a musical instrument or voices. If one were playing in a large room or a cathedral, where there were no carpets, insulation, this would happen. Carpets, curtains and other sound absorbing materials would give a clear clarity of sound. *Reverb* is an abbreviation.

Rhapsodie *(Fr.)* **Rhapsody** *(Eng.)* A free irregular form of composition.

Rhythm The pulsation of music. The division of musical ideas into regular metrical portion

Rhythm Machines contain realistic Drum Sounds which indicate Rhythm styles as $3/4$, $4/4$, Bossa Nova, Country, Disko, Rock, Slow Rock, and others. Supplementary controls to these may be Arpeggio, Fill In and Intro/Ending, Start/Stop, Tempo, Variation and Volume.

Ribbon Microphone Dynamic microphone using thin metal ribbon, between poles of a magnet. These are bidirectional and most fragile.

Rigaudon *(Fr.)* A lively French dance.

Rigore, Rigoroso *(It.)* In strict time.

Rimbombamento *(It.)* Resounding, booming.

Rinforzando, Rinforzare, Rinforzato, Rinforzo *(It.)* A reinforcement of the tone, or expression; indicating that either a single note or chord, or several notes are to be played with emphasis, although not with the suddenness of a *sforzando.*

Ripetizione *(It.)* Repetition.

Risoluto *(It.)* Resolved, resolute, bold.

Rit., Ritard: *(It.)* Abbreviations of Ritardando.

Ritardando *(It.)* Delaying the time gradually.

Riten. *(It.)* An abbreviation of *Retenuto.*

Ritenendo, Ritenente, Ritenento, Ritenuto *(It.)* Holding back time.

Ritornel, Ritornello *(It.)* **Ritournelle** *(Fr.)* The chorus or refrain of a song. Also a short prelude or introduction to an air, and the postlude that follows an air. It also applies to tutti parts before, between and after a solo passage in a concerto.

Roccoco, Rococo Old fashioned, odd, quaint.

Rohr *(Ger.)* Reed, pipe.

ROM *Read Only Memory* This part of the computer's memory is used to permanently store programs where contents can be read but not altered. ROM is usually used to store low level operating routine. These are factory presets *(see Sound Module).*

Romance *(Fr.)* **Romanza** *(It.)* **Romanze** *(Ger.)* An irregular romantic melody suggestive of a love story.

Rondeau *(Fr.)* **Rondo** *(It.)* A composition consisting of one prominent theme which appears again and again in alternation with other contrasting themes.

Root The fundamental note of any chord.

Rosalia *(Lat.)* The repetition of a passage several times over. Each time it is on a different degree of the staff.

Rota *(It.)* A wheel.

Rotondo *(It.)* Round, full.

Roulade *(Fr.)* A florid vocal passage. A division or rapid series of notes using one syllable.

Round A canon in unison or octave. A vocal composition in three or more parts, all written in the same clef, each singing their part in succession.

Roundel, Roundelay A type of rustic song or ballad. It constantly returns to the first verse.

Rubato *(It.)* Robbed, stolen. Part of the time values of certain tones are taken and given to another.

Rullando, Rullante *(It.)* Rolling on drum or tambourine.

Run A rapid passage of notes introduced as embellishment or part of the composition.

Russe *(Fr.)* Russian.

Rustico *(It.)* Rural, rustic, pastoral.

S

S Abbreviation for segno *(sign),* senza *(without),* sinistra *(left),* subito *(suddenly).*

Sackbut Old bass wind-instrument with a slide similar to a trombone.

Saiten *(Ger.)* Strings of a violin, guitar.

Saltando *(It.)* Leaping, proceeding by skips or jumps.

Saltarella, Salterella *(It.)* An Italian or Roman dance, very quick, skipping in character and usually in 2/4 or 6/8 time.

Salto *(It.)* A leap or skip.

Sample A sound digitally recorded from an acoustic instrument, as a piano(s), organ, group of instruments, whistles, noises which can be stored on a disk, a *ROM* card or a sampling keyboard.

Sampler A synthesizer or sound module that records and plays back sampled sounds produced by a real acoustical instrument. It is an audio device that converts sound into digital information that can be controlled by the computer.

Sanft *(Ger.)* Soft, mild, smooth.

Sans *(Fr.)* Without.

Saraband *(Eng.)* **Sarabanda** *(It.)* **Sarabande** *(Fr. and Ger.)* A dance said to be of Spanish or Oriental origin, slow and stately in character; a part of the classic suite.

Sarrusophone A brass wind instrument with double reed.

Satz *(Ger.)* Musical passage; theme or movement.

Saving To A Disk A performer, a creator puts performance, creations on a formatted disk so it is not lost or erased.

Sax-horn Cylinder brass wind-instrument with 3, 4 or 5 cylinders.

Saxophone A metal wind-instrument with a single reed and a mouthpiece similar to that of the clarinet.

Scale The succession of tones upon which any music is constructed. The Diatonic scale is either Major or Minor. The Minor scales are either Natural, Harmonic or Melodic. The Major and Minor scales employ both whole and half-steps. The Chromatic scale consists of half-steps only. The Whole-tone scale consists of whole steps only.

Scat Singer is a singer (vocalist) that sings what he/she feels within. It would be music without words (see Improvisation, *Rap Music).*

Scherz *(Ger.)* Scherzo *(It.)* Play, sport, joke, jest.

Scherzando, Scherzante, Scherzevole *(It.)*, **Scherzhaft** *(Ger.)* Playful, lively, sportive, merry.

Schlag *(Ger.)* A stroke or beat.

Schleifer *(Ger.)* Slurred note.

Schluss *(Ger.)* The end, conclusion.

Schnell, Schnelle *(Ger.)* Quick, rapid.

Schottisch *(Ger.)* A modern dance, rather slow in 2/4 time.

Schreibart *(Ger.)* Style; manner of composing.

Schule *(Ger.)* A school, or method for learning an instrument.

Schwach *(Ger.)* Piano, soft, weak.

Scherz *(Ger.)* Scherzo *(It.)* Play, sport, joke, jest.

SCMS refers to *Serial Copy Management System.* It disallows copies to be made of a digital to a digital recording. To avoid this when copying your own material transfer material using the professional digital disk using AES/EBU digital interfaces.

Scordare *(It.)* Out of tune.

Scordatura *(It.)* A different tuning of a string instrument.

Score The whole instrumentation and vocal parts of a composition, written on separate staves, placed under each other. Sometimes called a *chart.*

Score, piano Where the orchestral parts, or vocal parts are arranged to be played on the piano; an arrangement of music for piano.

Scoring Arranging the different parts of a composition for instruments and (or) voices on manuscript paper as a score.

Scorrendo *(It.)* Gliding from one sound to another.

Scotch scale. This scale omits the fourth and seventh degrees. Example: C-D-E-G-A-C.

SCSI The interface for choosing a sampler hard-disk access. Samplers use the speed of SCSI to load samples (See *SMDI*).

Sdegno *(It.)* Anger, wrath, passion.

Se *(It.)* If, as, provided, in case.

Sec *(Fr.)* Secco *(It.)* Dry, unornamented, plain, coldly.

Sechs *(Ger.)* Six.

Second An interval of one degree, as D to E, E to F.

Seconda *(It.)* Second.

Section A complete, but not an independent musical idea.

Secular music An expression used in opposition to sacred music. It is music for the theatre, concert, enjoyment.

Segno *(It.)* The sign. 𝄋 *al segno:* return to the sign; *dal segno* repeat from the sign.

Segue, Seguito *(It.)* Follows, now follows. Go on in a similar, or like manner.

Seguidilla *(Spa.)* A Spanish dance in triple time.

Sehr *(Ger.)* Very, much, extremely.
Sei *(It.)* Six.
Semi *(Lat.)* Half.
Semibreve *(Eng. and It.)* A whole note.

Whole Note & Rest

Semidemisemiquaver A sixty-fourth note.

64th Note & Rest

Semiquaver A sixteenth note.

16th Note & Rest

Semitono *(Eng.)* Semitonium *(Lat.)* A half-tone.
Semplice *(It.)* Simple, pure, plain.
Sempre *(It.)* Always, continually.
Sensibile *(It.)* Expressive; with feeling.
Sensible *(Fr.)* Leading note. Major seventh of scale.
Sentimentale, **Sentimento** *(It.)* Feeling, sentiment, delicate
 expression.
Senza *(It.)* Without.
Senza Ripetizione *(It.)* without repetition.
Se piace *(It.)* At will; at pleasure.
Septet *(Eng.)* **Septetto** *(It.)* A composition for seven voices or
instruments.

7th Interval

Septieme *(Fr.)* Septime *(Ger.)* The interval of a seventh.
Septimole, **Septiole** *(Lat.)* A group of seven notes, having the value,
and to be played in the time of four or six, of the same species. (see
Tuplet).

Septiole

Septuplets A group of seven notes (see *Tuplet).*
Sequence *(Eng. and Fr.)* Sequenz *(Ger.)* Sequenza *(It.)* A repetition of a
progression of chords or a melodic phrase or figure at a different
pitch.
Sequencer permits one to record a song, part of a song and play along
with it. Example; record the melody and play accompaniment
with it, or vice versed. It plays back information as *MIDI* data.
Sequencer software allows a computer to record *MIDI* data as a
multi-track tape recorder.
Sextuplets A group of six notes (see *Sextole, Tuplet).*

Sextuplet

SCSI - *Small Computer System Interface* Industry standard for
connecting peripheral devices to personal computers; up to seven SCSI
devices can be daisy chained to a Macintosh computer (See *SCSI).*

Serenade *(Fr.)* Serenata *(It.)* An evening concert in the open air at night.

Sereno *(It.)* Serene, calm, tranquil.

Seria, Serioso *(It.)* Serious, grave.

Sestet *(Eng.)* Sestetto *(It.)* Sextetto. A composition for six voices or instruments.

Sette *(It.)* Seven.

Settima, Settimo *(It.)* Interval of a seventh (see *Septieme).*

Severamente, Severita *(It.)* Severity, strictness.

Sexta *(Lat.)* Sixth.

Sextole, Sextuplet *(Lat.)* A group of six notes, having the value, and played in the time of four (see *Sextuplets & Tuplet).*

Sforza *(It.)* Forced; with force and energy.

Sforzando, Sforzato *(It.)* Forced; one particular chord or note to be played with force and emphasis.

Shako   A Trill.

Sharp   The sign which raises the pitch of a note one half step (see *Accidentals).*

Sharp, double   The sign which raises the pitch of a note one whole step (see *Accidentals).*

Shift   A change in position of the left hand in playing a string instrument.

Shotgun Microphones are directional microphones which are great for dialog on a movie set, where background sounds can be isolated.

Si   The name of the seventh degree of the major scale in solfeggio. In France and Italy the note "B" is called "Si."

Si bemol *(Fr.)* Si bemolle *(It.)* The note B flat.

Si bemol majeur *(Fr.)* Key of B flat major.

Si bemol mineur *(Fr.)* Key of B flat minor.

Siciliana, Siciliano *(It.)* A dance of the Sicilian peasants, a graceful movement of a slow, soothing, pastoral character, usually in 6/8 or 12/8 time.

Siegeslied *(Ger.)* A triumphal song.

Signature, key *(Eng.)* **Signatura** *(Spa.)* **Signatur** *(Ger.)* The name given to the flats and sharps placed at the beginning of a piece and at the beginning of each staff to indicate the key in which it is written.

Signature   A music signature or theme used to identify a Television or radio program. Usually it is played at the beginning and end.

Signature, time   The figures in the form of a fraction, placed at the beginning of a piece to indicate the number of beats to a measure and the kind of note which receives one beat or count.

Si majeur *(Fr.)* Key of B major.

Simile *(It.)* In like manner.

Si mineur *(Fr.)* Key of B minor.

Sinfonia *(It.)* Sinfonia *(Fr.)* An orchestral composition in many parts.

Sing-spiel *(Ger.)* Drama mixed with songs as opera and melodrama.

Siniestra *(Spa.)* Sinistra *(Lat.)* The left hand.

Sin, Sino *(It.)* To; as far as; until.

Sixth An interval of six diatonic degrees.

Skip A melodic interval that exceeds a whole tone.

Slargando, Slargandosi *(It.)* Extending, enlarging. The time to become gradually slower.

Slave A device that responds to commands from another which are in the system. This takes place in using a combination of MIDI instruments.

Slur *(Ger., legatobogen; Fr., liaison; It., legatura.)* A curved line placed over or under two or more notes indicating that they are to be connected smoothly, not detached. The slur is also used to indicate phrasing.

Smaniante, Smaniato, Smanioso *(It.)* Furious, vehement.

SMDI The acronym for *Musical Data Interchange*. It is a method of using *SCSI*, *Small Computer Interface*, to transfer information between computers and samplers.

Smaniante *(It.)* frantic with rage.

Sminuendo, Sminuito, Smorendo *(It.)* Diminishing; decreasing; gradually softer.

Smorzando, Smorzato (It.) Softer and slower; dying away.

SMF Refers to the Standard MIDI File. It is known as the only file format that most notation programs and sequencers have in common.

SMPTE *Society of Motion Picture and Television Engineers* developed a digital code which is used to synchronize film or video with computers, tape recorders and sequences. The standard time code which drops a frame number :0 and :01 each minute, except every 10th minute which compensates for *NTSC* variance from Real Clock Time (see *Macintosh Computer)*.

SMPTE Time Code is an eight digit address code used to identify each videotape frame by the hour, minute, second and frame number for precision editing.

Society of Motion Picture and Television Engineers (see *SMPTE)*.

Soave *(It.)* Played in a gentle, soft engaging style.

Software Used by a computer.

Sol In Solfeggio, the fifth tone of the scale. In France and Italy, *Sol* is always G.

Sol bemo *(Lat.)* The note G flat.

Sol bemol majeur *(Fr.)* Key of G flat major.

Sol bemol mineur *(Fr.)* Key of G flat minor.

Sol diese *(Fr.)* The note G sharp.

Sol diese mineur *(Fr.)* Key of G sharp minor.

Sol-fa To sing with syllables.

Solfaing Singing the notes of the scale to the monosyllables; do, re, mi, fa, so, la, si, do.

Solfege *(Fr.)* Solfeggi, Sofeggio *(It.)* Vocal exercises in which the notes sung are based on Solfaing.

Solo *(It., Fr., and Ger.)* A composition for a single voice, vocal or instrumental. A feature on a mixing console that reroute selected channels so the user can hear individual channels while the full mix plays.

Soloist A musician performs alone, with/without accompaniment.

Solo Voices A solo, monophonic, mono voice, meaning a one voice instrument as Trombone, Clarinet, Violin, and others. Included with these instruments there would be additional controls (companion) as to Chorus, Portamento, Pitch Blend, Stereo, Sustain, Vibrato.

Son *(Fr. and Spa.)* Sound.

Sonata *(It.)* Sonate *(Fr. and Ger.)* An instrumental composition, usually in three or four movements, each with a unity of its own, but all related to form a whole.

Sonatina *(It.)* **Sonatine** *(Fr.)* A short easy sonata, usually in two or three movements.

Song A vocal musical expression with words. A term used for information on a computer music disk to name sequencer's data for each piece which includes the name, number, tempo, style and other important functions which save the song.

Song Position Pointer Refers to a MIDI sequence file by reading sync signals as FSK *(Frequency Shift Keying)* or *SMPTE* time codes which are recorded on a tape track. In this way one can start playing a sequence at a given location and keep it in sync with the tape.

Sonic pertains to the speed level of sound, which is about 1088 feet per second, through the air at sea level.

Sono *(It.)* Sound, tone.

Sonore *(Fr.)* Sonoro *(It.)* Sonorous, harmonious, resonant.

Sopra *(It.)* Above, upon, over, before.

Soprano *(It.)* The treble; the highest female voice; also a boy's voice.

Sorda *(It.)* Muffled, veiled tone.

Sordamente *(It.)* Softly, gently; also damped, muffled.

Sordino *(It.)* Muted.

Sospirando, Sospirante, Sospirevole, Sospiroso *(It.)* Sighing, subdued.

Sostenendo, Sostenuto *(It.)* Sustaining the tone by keeping the notes vibrating for their full duration. Music terms signifying to hold a note *(sound)* as long as possible before playing the next note. There is a definite smoothness between sounds (see *Legato*).

Sotto *(It.)* Under, below.

Sotto voce *(It.)* Softly in a low voice; an undertone.

Sound A wave motion going through the air, that the human ear hears or detects. If it is not pleasant to the hearing, it is noise. The aspects to sound are the creation through soundwaves, the transmission through the air and the receiving by the human ear, or a microphone. Sound travels about 1,130 feet per second. The sound has certain characteristics, depending on the source as to the frequency, amplitude, envelope *(ADSR)*, harmonic content and phase (see *Amplitude*).

Sound-board A thin piece of resonant wood placed below the strings of an instrument to reinforce the tone.

Sound Libraries Collections of sounds put out by various manufactures. These may be on cards and disks that will expand the sound palette and variations of any *MIDI* instrument.

Sound Module A synthesizer without a keyboard that is controlled by an external MIDI Keyboard that will activate the sounds. Filters in a sound module can offer resonance. Many sound modules store waveforms in *Read Only Memory* (ROM) which cannot be erased. If one desires to use their own, or another source, one needs a sound module with *Random Access Memory (RAM)*.

Source A disk or folder that holds the original material to be copied or translated.

Space The intervals between the lines of the staff.

Special Interest Group (see *SIG*).

Speech Recognition An attached microphone picks up speech, music, or external sounds. On certain computers, one can hear a playback. On others, speech may be converted to text.

Spianato *(It.)* Smooth, even, legato.

Spiccato *(It.)* Detached. In violin music the notes are played with the point of the bow.

Spirito *(It.)* Spirit, life, energy.

Splits Allows one to assign different sounds to different layers on a keyboard. This allows one to play a choice of bass sounds in the left hand while playing a piano, clarinet, violin sound in the right hand. With a drum kit used in a split, each key would have a different sound.

Squillante *(It.)* Clear, plain, sounding, ringing.

Stabile *(It.)* Firm.

Staccato *(It.)* Detached, distinct, separated. Opposite of legato.

Staff or **Stave** The five horizontal, parallel lines, with the four spaces on which the notes are written.

Standing waves, see *Flutter echo.*

Standard MIDI File see *SMF.*

Standards, see *Classical Music.*

Stanza *(It.)* A verse of a song or hymn.

Stem The line attached to a note—head.

Stentando *(It.)* Heavy and retarding.

Stentato *(It.)* Hard, forced, loud.

Step Time Recording, or inputting music information, one note at a time.

Stereo A two channel sound.

Step A degree used on the staff. A step is a tone and a half-step is a semi-tone.

Stéso *(It.)* Extended.

Stéso móto *(It.)* A slow movement.

Stesso *(It.)* The same.

Stile, Stilo *(It.)* Style.

Sting In video lingo it is a brief vocal or instrumental passage that may serve as a slogan or an identifiable motif.

Stinguendo *(It.)* Dying away.

Stomp Boxes are floor effect pedals which is a tone enhancer usually made for guitarists or bassists. These can be classified as compressor/limiter, delay, distortion/overdrive, modulation effect, multi-effect, volume and other pedal types. Many effects can be created with these.

Stop On a string instrument, it means pressure on the string or strings. In organ terms, it is the rank or set of Organ-pipes similar in tone and quality.

Strain A part of a composition, a song, a theme, a tune or melody.

Strascicando, Strascicato *(It.)* Dragging the time.

Strepitoso *(It.)* Noisy.

Stress Refers to *Structural Engineering Systems Solver* which is a problem oriented language. It also refers to a music note, or a group of notes to be emphasized or to stand out, an accent.

Stretta *(It.)* A closing passage taken in quicker time.

Stretto *(It.)* Pressed together; faster. In a fugue, it is the part where the subject and answer overlap one another.

String Instruments may refer to a violin section (upper strings), 'cello section (lower strings), or any instrument that sounds when a string is set into vibration. These sounds may be programmed into the sequencer by a Sampler (see *Sample* and *Sampler).*

Striping A process of recording a signal to a tape track, from the beginning to end. If this is done before other entrances are made on the tape, it is called "prestriping". (see *FSK, SMPTE).*

Stringendo *(It.)* Pressing, accelerating the time.

Strisciando *(It.)* Gliding, slurring.

Stromenti *(It. pl.)* Musical instruments.

Strong *(Ger.)* Strict, severe, rigid.

Stück *(Ger.)* Piece, air, tune. **Stücken** *(Ger.)* Pieces, **Stück** *(Ger.)* Studies.

Stuonáre *(It.)* Singing out of tune.

Su *(It.)* Above, upon.

Suave *(It., Spa. and Fr.)* Sweet, mild, agreeable.

Sub *(Lat.)* Under, below, beneath.

Subdominant The fourth note of any scale or key.

Súbito *(It.)* Suddenly; immediately; at once.

Subject A melody or theme.

Submediant The sixth tone of a scale.

Submix, see *Overdub.*

Subtonic Under the tonic.

Suite *(Fr.)* A series of movements of a contrasting musical themes.

Suite do danses *(Fr.)* A set of dances generally known as a Suite.

Suivez *(Fr.)* Follow, attend, pursue.

Súl, Sull', Sulla *(It.)* On, upon the.

Súl A On the A string.

Súl D On the D string.

Súlla ponticello *(It.)* On or near the bridge.

Super *(Lat.)* Above, over.

Super-Bit Mapping A way of encoding 20 bit digital audio information for playback on standard 16-bit compact discs.

Superdominant Sixth degree of the scale.

Supertonic Second degree of the scale.

Sur *(It. and Fr.)* On, upon, over.

Suspension The holding over of any note of the preceding chord, into the chord that follows, therefore often producing a discard.

Symphonic An electronic animation that gives the impression that a large number of instruments are playing together.

Symphonie *(Fr. and Ger.)*, **Symphony** *(Eng.)* An orchestral composition of several movements.

Symphonious Harmonious agreement with sound.

Sync A short term for *synchronization* which represents a timing value. "*c*" is a device that generates timely sync pulsations for use in video components in its system. It is matching of sound to picture.

Synchronization Where more than one action is taking place at the same time and held together by a common factor. In music, this would be the steadiness of a beat.

Synchronous Modem carries the timing information with data.

Synchronization Royalties When royalties are paid to publishers whenever their song is used in a film, television show or commercials. These are called *Sync fees.* Publishers may charge what ever they may agree on. It is not a set figure.

Synchronous Terminal Refers to a data terminal that operates at a fixed rate with a transmitter and receiver in synchronization.

Synchronous Transmission Where data bits are sent at a fixed rate, with the transmitter and receiver synchronized. *Synchronous Transmission* eliminates the need for start and stop bits.

Syncopated *(Eng.)* A contraction of a note by cutting off part of its value and giving it to the next note.

Syncopation A shifting of an accent from a strong beat to a weak beat.

Sync Start In reference to a MIDI keyboard, it will synchronize the start, the start of a style when a key is pressed. Different keyboards have their own functions and may differ.

Sync Stop Causes a style on a MIDI keyboard to stop on the release of a key. Different keyboards have their own functions and may differ.

Synthesizer (Synthesis) Electronic keyboards that have facilities for construction of original and artificial sounds and effects as well as preset (factory) sounds. Sounds are created electronically generated waveforms along with signal processors. It may also pertain to software for creating sound effects through a computer (see *Sample, Sampler).*

Synthesis Algorithm A computer program or a set of computations designed to generate music.

Sweetening Singers adding a new or variant track (new notes or harmony) over the original. See *Tweaking.*

T

T An abbreviation of Tasto, Tempo, Tenor, Toe (in organ music) and Tutti.

Tablature *(Fr.)* A general term used for all the signs and characters used in writing music.

Table d'harmonie *(Fr.)*, **Table d'instrument** *(Fr.)* Sounding board or belly of an instrument.

Table-songs Songs for male voices which were very popular in German glee clubs.

Tabor A small drum used to accompany the pipes or fife in dances.

Tabret A form of drum used by ancient Hebrews.

Tacet *(Lat.)* **Tace, Taci, Taciasi** *(It.)* Silent.

Tact-führer *(Ger.)* Orchestra conductor.

Tactus *(Lat.)* In ancient music, a stroke of the hand in which the time was measured or beaten.

Tacet *(Lat.),* **Táce** *(It.),* **Táci** *(It.)* **Taciási** *(It.)* Silent, do not play.

Tact, Takt *(Ger.)* Time, measure.

Tact-pause *(Ger.)* A measure rest.

Tag An announcement at beginning or end of a commercial, with added information. If a tag is added to music, it would extend the length of a song.

Takt, see *Tact.*

Tambouret *(Fr.)* **Tambourine** *(Eng.)* A small percussion instrument, similar to the head of a drum, with little bells around the rim to increase the excitement of sound.

Tambourin *(Fr.)* A dance accompanied by the Tambourine. It is also a Tambourine.

Tam-tam A gong.

Tangent *(Ger.)* The *jack* of a harpischord. It plucks the string.

Tanto *(It.)* So much, as much.

Tantum ergo *(Lat.)* A hymn sung at the benediction in the Roman Catholic service.

Tanz A German dance.

Tanz-kunst *(Ger.)* The art of dancing.

Tárdo *(It.)* Slow.

Taste *(Ger.)* **Tásto** *(It.)* The touch of any instrument.

Tasten-brett *(Ger.)* The keyboard of a piano.

Technique The technical side of playing or singing.

Tema *(It.)* A theme or subject; a melody.

Temperament The tuning of a piano by dividing the octave into twelve semi-tones. This system is called *equal temperament.*

Tempered Having a perfect adjustment of sounds.

Tempestóso Stormy and boisterous.

Tempête *(Fr.)* Boisterous dance in 2/4 time.

Template A publication *sample* that provides the structure and layout for other corresponding publications. This shows the visual part of the architecture of a digital synthesizer as it is shown on a computer screen during a *patch editing* process (see *Style Sheet).*

Témpo *(It.)* Time; the rate of movement.

Témpo alla breve *(It.),* Cut time or a quick pace.

Témpo a piacére *(It.),* Timing at pleasure.

Témpo cómodo *(It.),* Easy moderate degree of movement.

Témpo di bállo *(It.)* In dance time, rather fast in tempo.

Témpo di cappélla *(It.)* Usually $4/2$ or more commonly used as

$2/2$, Alla Bréve rhythm marked as ¢.

Témpo di gavótta *(It.)* In the time of a Gavot.

Témpo di menuétto *(It.)* In the time of a minuet.

Témpo di polácca *(It.)* In the time of a Polacca.

Témpo di valse *(It.)* In the time of a waltz.

Témpo frettévole/frettolóso *(It.)* In a quicker, hurried time.

Témpo giústo *(It.)* In exact strict time.

Témpo ordinário *(It.)* Referred to as tempo minore and témpo alla semibreve all in 4/4 time with notes having their correct values.

Témpo perdúto *(It.)* Interrupted, irregular time.

Témpo primo *(It.)* In the first or original tempo.

Témpo reggiáto *(It.)* The time to be accommodated by a soloist.

Témpo rubáto *(It.)* The retardation *(slower)* or acceleration of a measure *(faster)*, or several measures. It is a release from strict time.

Témpo wie vorher *(Ger.)* In the time as before.

Tendre *(Fr.)* Tender.

Tenebrae *(Lat.)* Darkness. It is a name given to the Roman Catholic service during Holy Week in commemoration of the crucifixion.

Teneramént, Tenerézza, Ténero *(It.)* Tenderly, softness, delicacy.

Ténero *(It.)* Tenderly, softly and delicate.

Tenir *(Fr.)* To hold the bow of a stringed instrument.

Tenor The high natural male voice.

Tenor clef The C clef when placed on the fourth line.

Tenóre di grázia *(It.)* Delicate and graceful tenor voice.

Tenóre robústo A strong tenor voice.

Tenóre secóndo Second tenor.

Tenúto *(It.),* **Tenúte** *(It.)* Held, sustained. (Abbreviation *Ten.*)

Teoría *(It.)* Theory.

Teoría del cánto *(It.)* Theory or art of singing.

Terpsichore Classical mythology, the muse of choral dance an song.

Tertia *(Lat.),* **Tertzia** *(Ger.)* Third, tierce. An organ stop sounding a third or tenth above the foundation stops.

Terz decimole *(Ger.)* A group of thirteen notes having the time value of eight, or twelve similar ones.

Terz-flöte *(Ger.)* A flute sounding a minor third above, also an organ stop.

Tetrachord *(Gr.)* Tetracordo *(Fr.),* Tetracordo *(It.)* A fourth; a scale series of four notes.

Theme A subject; a tune on which variations are made.

Theorbe *(Ger.)* Theorbo *(Eng.)* An old stringed instrument, looking and sounding like a lute. It was used for accompanying singers during the seventeenth century. Employing two necks, the longest contained the bass strings.

Theory The science of music.

Theremin One of the first, if not the first truly electronic music instrument. It was created by the Russian inventor, Dr. Leon Theremin years ago and was introduced to this country in 1927 by RCA. *(NOTE:)The author of this Dictionary was very fortunate to have heard and seen it in its infancy while still in Grade School. It was a matter of moving one hand close to one oscillating circuit vertical antenna for pitch sounds (melody) and the other hand close to another oscillating circuit horizontal antenna which controlled the volume.*

Third An interval of three diatonic degrees. This could be defined as going from one space to the next higher or lower space on a music staff, or one line to the very next line, higher or lower from a given note.

Through A special line or cable connected to a computer, going to a MIDI, going to a printer, going to an amplifier or several amplifiers.

Thorough bass It is a system of Harmony that employs figured bass.

Threnodia *(Lat.)*, **Threnodie** *(Gr.)* An elegy, a funeral song.

Threnody Lamentation.

Thru Box (see: *MIDI Thru*)

Thumb-string The melody string of a banjo.

Tie A curved line above or below two or more notes of the pitch which indicate that they are played like one note equal in length to the two or more.

Tie

Tierce de Picardie *(Fr.)* A composition in a minor mode that ends with a major chord.

Timbal *(Spa.)*, **Timbale** *(Fr.)*, **Timbállo** *(It.)* Kettle drum.

Timballes *(Fr.)* Kettledrums.

Timbre The quality of a musical tone played by various instruments (see, *Harmonic Series*).

Timbrel Refers to the ancient Hebrew instrument likened to a tambourine.

Time The division of sound within a measure(s).

Time Code This is the method of synchronizing *MIDI* devices with the audio or visual devices when using a prerecorded or generated electronic pulse. In reference to a videotape duration, concerning the hours, minutes, seconds and frames that a tape lasts, an electrical counter or index is used. It is usually burnt in the tape when being logged during *Offline editing*. This marking is usually visible with a special time code reader (see *Click Track, FSK, SMPTE*).

Timidezza, con *(It.)* With timidity.

Timorosaménte *(It.)* Timidly with fear.

Timoróso *(It.)* Timorous with some hesitation.

Timpani *(It. and Spa.)* Kettledrums (see *Timbal, Timballes*).

Tirato *(It.)* Down-bow.

Tira tútto *(It.)* A mechanism on an organ which acts on all stops thus enables the performer to obtain the full power contained within the instrument.

Toccata *(It.)* An old form of composition in a free, bold and brilliant style for Harpsichord, Organ or Piano.

Toccatina *(It.)* A short toccata.

Todeslied *(Ger.)* A dirge, funeral song.

Todtenlöckchen *(Ger.)* Funeral bell.

Todtenlied *(Ger.)* Funeral song or anthem.

Tonal Range Refers to the lowest and the highest note that can be sung or played on a musical instrument by a performer. In photography, or a printing process, it would be the brightest and the darkest tone, or color in a picture or in print.

Tóndo *(It.)* Round or full tone.

Tone The sound and quality of a voice or instrument.

Tone, whole An interval consisting of two half-tones.

Tone Generator The heart and function of a modular keyboard system. Sounds generated can include percussion, all voices of a full orchestra, keyboard and acoustical piano sounds through **AWM** *(Advanced Wave Memory)*, FM *(Frequency Modulation),* and WM *(Wave Memory)* for Organ Combinations. A Tone Generator is a **M**usic Synthesizer. It can provide musical instrument sounds along with reverberation, flanging, phasing to delay, wah-wah, panning, chorus, tremolo, vibrato, activation of keyboard pressure, velocity-sensitivity, volume, timbre and degrees of sensitivity.

Tone Programs Consists of Piano, Electronic Piano, Harpsichord, Clavier, Music Box, Celesta, Organ, Guitars, Strings, Orchestra, Voice, Trumpet, Trombone, Clarinet, Drums and many more.

Tongue A thin elastic slip of metal in an organ pipe that vibrates to produce a sound.

Tonguing A way of articulating notes on flute, trumpet, trombone.

Tonic, Tónica *(It.),* **Tonica** *(Ger.),* **Tonique** *(Fr.)* The key note of any scale.

Tonic The keynote of a scale.

Tonic Sol-Fa The Movable-Do system of teaching vocal music. The syllables used are; doh, ray, me, fah, soh, lah and te.

Touch The style of striking, or pressing the keys of a piano, organ or other keyboard instrument.

Touch Tone Enables fine control of volume and timbre on a keyboard. The *Initial Touch* sound control is determined by the amount of pressure, or speed in which the key is pressed. The *After Touch* is determined by the amount of subsequent pressure on the keyboard, after being pressed.

Track The recording or sound portion of video or film. It consists of one or more lines of music, sounds or information on a disk that requires very little space which is a digital signal ("0" or "1"). A full disk would have many single tracks on it. It is the pathway of a input signal on film, tape or disk It stores information.

Tracks Digital signals on a hard or floppy disk as on a audio tape, a recording space. On an audio tape, there is a continuous variable signal representing a sound wave. This is the *analog* signal. On a hard or floppy disk there is either a maximum signal or nothing at all. This is the *digital* signal. When recording on a sequencer, it is possible each instrument may be recorded on a different track. When obtaining a playback through the MIDI, one assigns a different channel for each instrument that goes through the sound generator that is assigned. It stores information that has been programmed.

Track-To-Track Seek Time The length of time required to move from one track to another.

Trait de chant *(Fr.)* A melodic passage or phrase.

Trait d'harmonie *(Fr.)* A succession or sequence of chords.

Transpose Changing one key to another key.

Transposition using a computer is simple. Chromatic transposition moves all selected notes to any interval desired - up a seventh, lowered a third, etc. Diatonic transposition move or shifts the selected notes by the same lines and spaces. Enharmonic transposition maintains the pitches of the selected notes but changes name. Modal transposition keeps selected notes or pitches on the same lines and spaces but changes the necessary accidentals This could be from going from minor to major, or major to minor.

Tranquillo *(It.)* Tranquillity, calmness, quietness.

Transcription An arrangement for any instrument of a song or other composition, not originally written for that instrument; an adaptation.

Transposed Changed to another key.

Treble Soprano; the upper or highest voice.

Treble clef The soprano, or G clef (see *Clef*).

Tremolando, Tremolate, Tremulo, Tremulo *(It.)* Trembling, quivering. Rapid alternation of the tones of a chord.

Tremolo simulates the sound of a rotating speaker system. It is a wavering of sound by an instrumental voice. This can be a slow or fast speed controlled by the user.

Transducer Appliance that transforms energy from one form to another.

Triad A chord of three notes; Root, third and fifth.

Trill *(Ger.,* **Triller**; *Fr.,* **Trille**; *It.,* **Trillo**; *Eng.,* **Shako**; *Spa* **Trino**) A shake. The rapid alternation of two tones, either a half-tone or a whole tone apart.

Trio *(It.)* A piece for three instruments or voices.

Triphony Three sounds heard together.

Triplice *(It.)* Triple, threefold and treble.

Triplet A group of three notes played in the time of two similar ones (see *Tuplet).*

Triton *(Fr.)* **Tritone** *(Eng.)* **Tritono** *(It.)* **Tritonus** *(Lat.)* Interval of an augmented fourth.

Triumphirend, Triumphlied *(Ger.)* Song of triumph.

Tromba *(It.)* A trumpet. Eight foot organ stop.

Trombone A metal instrument of the trumpet family. It has a "U" shaped slide, adjustable to seven positions. Some have three piston valves rather than the slide.

Trommler *(Ger.)* A drummer.

Trommel-kasten *(Ger.)* The body of a drum.

Trommel-schläger, Trommel-klöpfel *(Ger.)* Drumstick.

Tróppo *(It.)* Too much. *non tróppo,* not too much.

Trompe de béarn *(Fr.)* Jews' harp.

Trumpet A metal wind-instrument with a cupped mouthpiece and a small bell. It has three piston valves.

Truncation Cutting off by trimming an excess. This could printing needs. In making a digital sample there could be "dead-time" which must be deleted before the sound occurs at the beginning of a sample or at the end of the sample.

Tuba Large metal wind instrument with a deep tone. It is the natural bass for all brass instruments. Some are now being made out of plastic material.

Tune Air; a melody.

Tuplet Irregular grouping of note values as triplets *(three notes of equal length),* quintuplets *(five notes of equal length,* sextuplets *(six notes of equal length)* septuplets *(seven notes of equal length).*

Turn Embellishment made from the note above and the note below the principal note.

Túrco *(It.)* In the style of Turkish music.

Tútte Tútti *(It.)* All, the entire orchestra or chorus.

Tútte fórza *(It.)* **Tútte la fórza** As loud as possible with utmost force and vehemence.

Tútte córde *(It.)* Release the soft pedal on the piano.

Tútte unísoni *(It.)* All in unison.

Tweaking Changing sounds, balance parts, set or adjust tempo, modifying. See *Sweetening.*

Tútto árco *(It.)* With the entire length of the bow.

Twelfth Organ stop tuned twelve notes above the diapasons.

Tweeter Loudspeaker that produces high frequencies.

Tympani *(It.)* Kettledrums.

U

Udíta, Udíto *(It.)* Sense of hearing.

Uditóre *(It.)* The listener.

Ueberblasen *(Ger.)* Overblowing.

Ueberschlagen *(Ger.)* Crossing of hands in keyboard playing.

Uebersetzen *(Ger.)* Passing a finger over the thumb. In organ pedal playing it is passing one foot over the other.

Uebergang *(Ger.)* Transition; change of key.

Uebereinstimmung *(Ger.)* Consonance, harmony.

Uebung *(Ger.)* Exercise or study.

Uguále *(It.)* Equal, like, similar.

Umfang *(Ger.)* Compass, extent.

Umfang der Stimme *(Ger.)* Compass of voice.

Umkehrung *(Ger.)* Inversion.

Umschreibung *(Ger.)* Limitation.

Umore *(It.)* Humor, playfulness.

Un, Una, Uno *(It.)* A, an, one.

Unaccompanied Without instrumental accompaniment.

Una corda *(It.)* One string; piano music, the soft pedal on the left side.

Unda maria *(Lat.)* Waving effect.

Unda maria *(Lat.)* Organ stop tuned flatter than others.

Ungerade Takt-art *(Ger.)* Triple or uneven time.

Ungezwungen *(Ger.)* Easily and naturally.

Unison Oneness of sound. Sounds of the same pitch or vibration.

Unsingbar *(Ger.)* Impossible to be sung.

Unter *(Ger.)* Under, below.

Unterhaltungs-stück *(Ger.)* Entertainment, amusing, a bright piece of music.

Unterricht *(Ger.)* Instruction, information.

Upbeat, see *Anacrusis.*

Ut *(Fr.)* The note C; the syllable originally applied by Guido to the note C, or do.

Ut bemol *(Fr.)* The note C flat.

Ut diese *(Fr.)* The note C sharp.

Ut diese mineur *(Fr.)* The key of C sharp minor.

Ut mineur *(Fr.)* C minor.

Ut queant laxis *(Lat.)* Beginning words of the *Hymn to St. John the Baptist.* It is said Guido took the syllables, *ut, re, mi, fa, sol, la* for his solfeggio on various degrees of the scale. In the Key of C, ut would be C; re would be D, mi would be E; fa would be F; sol would be G; and la would be A. (see *Tonic Sol-Fa*).

Ut supra *(Lat.)* As above; as before.

V

V An abbreviation for Verte, Violin, Volti, Voce.

Va *(It.)* Go on.

Vaccilando *(It.)* Wavering; uncertain; irregular in time.

Vago*(It.)* Vague; rambling; uncertain.

Valour *(Fr.)* Valore *(It.)* Length, duration of a note.

Valse *(Fr.)* A waltz; a dance in triple time.

Valve In brass instruments, it is a device to lengthen or shorten a tube to produce tones between the natural harmonics. There are usually three in number.

Vamp To improvise an accompaniment.

Variations Melodic, harmonic and rhythmic changes of a theme.

Vaudeville *(Fr.)* Usually a variety show.

VCA, see *Amplifier, Expander, Compressor.*

VDA, see *Amplifier.*

Velocity The amount of time between the initiation of a key attack on a music keyboard and the time it reaches the bottom of the keyboard bed which is determined by how hard a key is struck.

Velocity Microphone Another name for the *Ribbon Microphone.*

Velocity Sensitivity The quality of an instrument or MIDI software to determine note dynamics as a result of velocity information. It can respond to a players touch.

Veloce, Velocemente *(It.)* Swiftly; quickly; in a rapid time.

Ventil *(Ger.)* **Ventile** *(It.)* A valve in wind instruments.

Venusto *(It.)* Beautiful, gracefully.

Vepres (Fr.) Vespers; evening prayers.

Vergette, Verghetta *(It.)* Tail, or stem of a note.

Versette, Versetten *(Ger.)* Short pieces for the organ, intended as preludes, interludes, or postludes.

Versetzen *(Ger.)* Transpose.

Verso *(It.)* Verse.

Vertatur, Verte *(Lat.)* Turn over.

Verzierung *(Ger.)* Embellishment, ornament.

Vezzoso *(It.)* Graceful, sweet, tender.

Vibrato, Vibrato *(It.)* A strong, vibrating, full quality of tone.

Vibrato With a musical instrument, it can be wide or narrow as to the attitude of the performer. It is done by the movement of the hand on a string instrument, or a pulsation of ones lips on a woodwind or brass instrument. These are on assignment with a synthesizer.

Video Tape Tape on which both sound and picture are recorded simultaneously, versus audio tape which records only sound.

Vide *(Fr.)*, Vido *(It.)* Open.

Viol *(Ger.)* Much.

Vietáto *(It.)* Forbidden and prohibited.

Vier *(Ger.)* Four.

Vif *(Fr.)* Lively, brisk, quick.

Vigorosamente, Vigoroso *(It.)* Vigorous, bold, energetic.

Villageois *(Fr.)* Rustic.

Villancico, Villancio *(Spa.)* Pastoral poem or song.

Villanella *(It.)* Villanelle *(Fr.)* An old rustic Italian dance, accompanied with singing.

Vinate *(It.)* Drinking songs.

Viol An old string instrument resembling the violin with six strings and played with a bow.

Viola A tenor-violin. It is similar in tone and formation to the violin but larger in size. It is played with a bow.

Violin A well known stringed instrument. It has a brilliant tone, capable of every variety of expression. It has four strings and is played with a bow.

Violoncell *(Ger.)* **Violoncelle** *(Fr.)* **Violoncello** *(It.)* The large bass violin held between the knees while being played. It is often called the *Cello.*

Virgin A tape or disk that has never been recorded on.

Virginal A small keyed instrument, used much in the time of Queen Elizabeth. Usually it was placed on a table when played.

Virtuoso *(Ger.)* A skillful performer on some instrument.

Vista *(It.)* Sight.

VITC An acronym for **V**ertical **I**nterval **T**ime **C**ode. It is readable when the tape is moving or not moving. It is a signal recorded by rotary heads and recorded at the same time as the video signal. It can be striped either before or after the video picture is recorded. (See *SMPTE, striping).*

Vistamente, Vitamente *(It.)* Quickly, swiftly, immediately, briskly.

Vivace, Vivacemente *(It.)* Lively, briskly, quickly.

Vivacissimo *(It.)* Very lively.

Vive *(Fr.)* Lively, brisk, quick.

Vivo *(It.)* Animated, lively, brisk.

Vocal Belonging to the human voice

Voce *(It.)* The voice.

Voice The sounds produced by the vocal organs in singing. The human voices are classified from the lowest to the highest as follows: bass, baritone, tenor, alto, mezzo soprano and soprano. It is a sound generated by an instrument.

Voice Chip A single intergrated circuit which is the primary device for sound generating in a synthesizer.

Voice, falsetto Tones above natural range sung in artificial tone.

Voice Grade Line Channel that is capable of carrying voice frequency signals.

Voice Input A system that uses a microphone and interface to allow commands to the computer be carried out by a voice speaking into the microphone.

Voicing The regulation of the parts of an organ-pipe for the proper pitch and character of sound. With the piano, the hammer felt is needled, sometime sanded and ironed for better quality of sound..

Voix *(Fr.)* The voice.

Volante *(It.)* Flying; light rapid series of notes.

Volatine *(It.)* Short runs.

Volkslied *(Ger.)* A folk song.

Voll *(Ger.)* Full.

Volta *(It.)* Turn, time.

Volta prima *(It.)* First time.

Voltare *(It.)* To turn.

Volta seconda *(It.)* The second time.

Volteggiando, Volteggiare (It.) Crossing the hands.

Volti *(It.)* Turn over.

Volume Storage space which may be part of a disk, or the entire disk. It can be the quantity of fullness of tone from a voice or instrument. loudness or softness of a voice, or music coming from a speaker system or amplifier (see *Touch Tone*).

Voluntary An organ solo played before, during or after a church service.

Von *(Ger.)* By, of, from, on.

Vorspiel *(Ger.)* Prelude or introduction.

Vortrag *(Ger.)* Interpretation or style of performance.

Vox *(Lat.)* Voice.

Vue *(Fr.)* Sight.

Vuide *(Fr.)* Open.

W

WAH A specific effect assigned to a brass musical instrument by using a mute, or the hand in the bell of the instrument. The mute would be a *WAH WAH* mute which was a product of the Big or Name Band era. Its effect is remarkable on a synthesizer.

Waits An old word meaning oboes, oboe players, musicians performing at night in the open air.

Wald-flote *(Ger.)* Forest or shepherd's flute.

Waldhorn *(Ger.)* Forest-horn. Valveless French Horn.

Waltz A dance using music of triple measure. The tempo may vary from slow to fast. The waltz has been used as a symphonic movement.

Wassail   A merry or convivial song.

Wavetable Refers to a wavetable sample-based synthesis.

Wehmuth *(Ger.)* Sadness.

Weich *(Ger.)* Soft, gentle.

Weise *(Ger.)* Melody, air, song.

Weite Harmonie *(Ger.)* Open harmony.

Wenig *(Ger.)* Little.

Whole note A semibreve, the longest note used in modern notation.

Whole rest A pause equal in length to a whole note.

Whole tone A major second. Two semi-tones.

Wholetone scale A series of six consecutive whole steps. Example 1: C-D-E-F#-G#-A#-C   Example 2: Db-Eb-F-G-A-Cb-Db.

Wind-instruments The instruments where the sounds are produced by the breath, or by the wind of bellows.

Wolf A name applied to a discord when playing on certain keys on the piano, or organ when tuned in unequal temperament .

Woodwind The orchestral wind instruments that are made from wood.

Woofer A speaker made to produce low frequencies.

Workstation A keyboard that offers playback of sounds, a disk system for recording and editing audio utilizing a sequencer with all   multitimbral sound playback capabilities.

Wuchtig *(Ger.)* Weighty, ponderously.

Wurde *(Ger.)* Dignity.

Wuth *(Ger.)* Madness, rage.

X

Xylophone   An instrument consisting of a series of bars or blocks of wood tuned to the scale and played upon with mallets. It is a percussion instrument.

Y

Y Adapter or Connector A "Y" shaped cord that allows the output from one instrument to be channeled into two devices, or two instruments to be channeled into one device.

Yellow Book (see *CD-DA*).

Yodel or jodel The peculiar warbling of the Swiss and Tirolese peasants.

Z

Zampogna *(It.)* A bagpipe.

Zapatear *(Spa.)* Beating time with the foot.

Zargen *(Ger.)* Refers to the sides of a stringed instrument as a violin, viola, guitar.

Zart, Zärtlich *(Ger.)* Tenderly, softly, delicately.

Zarzuela *(Spa.)* A short dramatic performance with incidental songs, also meaning a comic opera or an operetta.

Zeichen *(Ger.)* A sign.

Zeitmass *(Ger.)* A measure, time.

Zeitmesser *(Ger.)* A metronome.

Zelosamente *(It.)* Zealously and ardently.

Zerstreute Harmonie *(Ger.)* Dispersed, or extended, harmony.

Ziehharmonica *(Ger.)* An accordion.

Ziemlich *(Ger.)* Rather.

Zierlich *(Ger.)* Neat, graceful.

Zierrathen *(Ger.)* Refers to ornaments.

Zingaresa *(It.)* In the style of gypsy music.

Zigeunermusik *(Ger.)* Gipsy music.

Zinken *(Ger.)* A family of obsolete wood wind instruments made by the Italians called cornetto. It is also a hollow-toned reed-stop in the organ, usually pitched at 8-feet.

Zisch *(Ger.)* Hiss.

Zither *(Ger.)* Sweet-toned instrument of about thirty strings and is plucked by the fingers. Some of the strings are used for the accompaniment.

Zitternd *(Ger.)* A trembling.

Zögernd *(Ger.)* Lingering, hesitating, a slackening of time.

Zolfa *(It.)* The same as Sol-fa.

Zoppa, Zoppe, Zoppo *(It.)* Lame, halting.

Zone A selected section of a MIDI keyboard defined by a lower and higher key. These Keyboard Zones can be assigned to a MIDI channel. Where two keyboard zones adjoin without overlapping, the division between them, would be called a "split point". Where zones overlap they are referred to as layers.

Zu *(Ger.)* At, by, in, to, into.

Zug *(Ger.)* A draw stop on an organ, harmonium, harpischord, the pedal of a piano or the slide of a trombone.

Zugtrompete *(Ger.)* A slide trumpet, *the soprano trombone.*

Zunehmend *(Ger.)* Increasing, crescendo.

Zungenblatt *(Ger.)* A clarinet reed.

Zurällig *(Ger.)* An accidental as sharps, flats and natural signs (see Accidentals).

Zurückhaltung *(Ger.)* Retardation.

Zurückhalten *(Ger.)* Retardation, slackening the time.

Zurückgehend *(Ger.)* Going back to the original time after a accelerando.

Zusammen *(Ger.)* Together.

Zusammengesetzt *(Ger.)* Compound as used in compound time.

Zwei *(Ger.)* Two.

Zweifach *(Ger.)* Double.

Zweifüssig *(Ger.)* Referring to two feet as applied to an organ pipe.

Zweigesang *(Ger.)* Duet.

Zweigestrichene Octave *(Ger.)* An octave or twice accented.

Zweihalbe Take *(Ger.)* 2/2 time.

Zweihändig *(Ger.)* For two hands.

Zweistimmig *(Ger.)* In two parts, for two voices or instruments

Zweiunddreissigstel *(Ger.)* Demisemiquaver.

Zweivierteltakt *(Ger.)* 2/4 time.

Zwischenraum *(Ger.)* Space between two lines of the stave.

Zwischensatz *(Ger.)* Episode or a part intervening between the development of a fugue.

Zwischenact *(Ger.)* Interval between the acts of a dramatic performance as an entr'acte.

Zwischenactmusik *(Ger.)* Music between the acts of a dramatic performance (see *Zwischensatz).*

Zwischenspiel *(Ger.)* Interlude.

Zwolf *(Ger.)* Twelve.

Zwölfachteltakt *(Ger.)* 12/8 time.

Zymase *(Ger.)* Cymbal.

CHORDS

Chords include a combination of three or more sounds, each played simultaneously. It is a process of building from a given note, usually called a Root. The Root is also the Chord Name. Notes added to the Chord name are inserted a third higher. If the Root is a note (sound) written on a space, the next space higher would be the next note or sound. Going up to the next space, by adding another note would add another sound to the root making three notes or sounds.

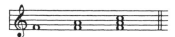

These three notes are classified as a Triad or a Chord. If one continues up the ladder to the next space, a four note or tone combination appears which is called a Seventh. Adding another note or sound to the next space gives one a Ninth Chord. Adding another note or sound to the next space creates an Eleventh Chord and still adding another note or sound to the next space gives one a Thirteenth Chord. If one continues there will be a duplication of notes. The same rules would apply if started with a lined note.

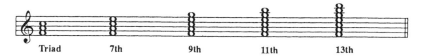

Any tone in a major or minor scale may be used as a Root. In building the chords as explained above, one would abide by the key signature being used in the chord construction. Triads or chords, either Major or Minor, are determined by the interval between the first two notes of the chord, as to whether they are a major or minor interval. Seventh chords have an interval of either a Major of Minor Seventh from the Root. The Seventh Chord containing the minor seventh from the Root would simply be known as a seventh chord (C7, G7, Bb7, *etc.*). The Seventh Chord containing a major seventh interval would be know as a Major Seventh Chord (Cmaj7, Cma7, CM, or CΔ). This idea prevails in the use of Ninth, Eleventh and Thirteenth Chords.

The most common chords are made from a diatonic major or a minor scale. If the tones in the chords are changed from the notes in the scale used, the chord is said to be *altered*.

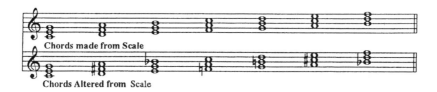

A chord is incomplete if one of the tones is missing. This usually happens in the use of the Ninth, Eleventh and Thirteenth Chords.

In using a chord, if the root (Chord Name) is the lowest tone of the chord, it is said to be in the Root or Fundamental Position. If another tone of the chord is used as the lowest sound, it becomes an inverted chord. The first inversion of a chord would have the Third of the chord as the lowest sound or note. The Second inversions would have the Fifth of the chord as the lowest sound or note, and the Third Inversion would have the Seventh of the chord as the lowest sound or note.

Where the same chord has two different names as *B or Cb,* or *C# or Db,* it is called an *Enharmonic* Chords. Although the chord spellings are different, the sounds will be the same. A "B Chord" spelled B-D#-F# would sound the same as a "Cb chord" spelled Cb-Eb-Gb.

A Double Sharp (⬟) raises the pitch of a note (sound) a whole step higher. A Double Flat (⬟) lowers the pitch of a note (sound) a whole step lower. A Sharp (⬟) raises the pitch of a note (sound) one half step higher. The Flat (⬟) lowers the pitch of a note (sound) one half step. The "+" sign is used to indicate an Augmented 5. It is also indicated to indicate the Augmented 9th the Augmented 11 (+11) and the Augmented 13th (+13). The degree mark (°) is used to indicate a Diminished Fifth (°5). At times one may see a -5 meaning a lowered or diminished Fifth. The following are further examples -3 (minor third), -9 (minor ninth) and -13 (minor thirteenth).

For further information on Chords, the author suggests obtaining his *CHORD DICTIONARY for All Keyboard Instruments* and *CHORD ENCYCLOPEDIA for All Instruments,* published by Kenyon Publications.

MAJOR CHORDS

Ab	=	Ab	-	C	-	Eb
A	=	A	-	C#	-	E
A#	=	A#	-	Cx	-	E#
Bb	=	Bb	-	D	-	F
B	=	B	-	D#	-	F#
Cb	=	Cb	-	Eb	-	Gb
C	=	C	-	E	-	G
C#	=	C#	-	E#	-	G#
Db	=	Db	-	F	-	Ab
D	=	D	-	F#	-	A
D#	=	D#	-	Fx	-	A#
Eb	=	Eb	-	G	-	Bb
E	=	E	-	G#	-	B
F	=	F	-	A	-	C
F#	=	F#	-	A#	-	C#
Gb	=	Gb	-	Bb	-	Db
G	=	G	-	B	-	D
G#	=	G#	-	B#	-	D#

MINOR CHORDS

Abm	=	Ab	-	Cb	-	Eb
Am	=	A	-	C	-	E
A#m	=	A#	-	C#	-	E#
Bbm	=	Bb	-	Db	-	F
Bm	=	B	-	D	-	F#
Cbm	=	Cb	-	Ebb	-	Gb
Cm	=	C	-	Eb	-	G
C#m	=	C#	-	E	-	G#
Dbm	=	Db	-	Fb	-	Ab
Dm	=	D	-	F	-	A
D#m	=	D#	-	F#	-	A#
Ebm	=	Eb	-	Gb	-	Bb
Em	=	E	-	G	-	B
Fm	=	F	-	Ab	-	C
F#m	=	F#	-	A	-	C#
Gbm	=	Gb	-	Bbb	-	Db
Gm	=	G	-	Bb	-	D
G#m	=	G#	-	B	-	D#

SEVENTH CHORDS

Ab7	=	Ab	-	C	-	Eb	-	Gb
A7	=	A	-	C#	-	E	-	G
A#7	=	A#	-	Cx	-	E#	-	G#
Bb7	=	Bb	-	D	-	F	-	Ab
B7	=	B	-	D#	-	F#	-	A
Cb7	=	Cb	-	Eb	-	Gb	-	Bbb
C7	=	C	-	E	-	G	-	Bb
C#7	=	C#	-	E#	-	G#	-	B
Db7	=	Db	-	F	-	Ab	-	Cb
D7	=	D	-	F#	-	A	-	C
D#7	=	D#	-	Fx	-	A#	-	C#
Eb7	=	Eb	-	G	-	Bb	-	Db
E7	=	E	-	G#	-	B	-	D
F7	=	F	-	A	-	C	-	Eb
F#7	=	F#	-	A#	-	C#	-	E
Gb7	=	Gb	-	Bb	-	Db	-	Fb
G7	=	G	-	B	-	D	-	F
G#7	=	G#	-	B#	-	D#	-	F#

MINOR SEVENTH CHORDS

Abm7	=	Ab	-	Cb	-	Eb	-	Gb
Am7	=	A	-	C	-	E	-	G
A#m7	=	A#	-	C#	-	E#	-	G#
Bbm7	=	Bb	-	Db	-	F	-	Ab
Bm7	=	B	-	D	-	F#	-	A
Cbm7	=	Cb	-	Ebb	-	Gb	-	Bbb
Cm7	=	C	-	Eb	-	G	-	Bb
C#m7	=	C#	-	E	-	G#	-	B
Dbm7	=	Db	-	Fb	-	Ab	-	Cb
Dm7	=	D	-	F	-	A	-	C
D#m7	=	D#	-	F#	-	A#	-	C#
Ebm7	=	Eb	-	Gb	-	Bb	-	Db
Em7	=	E	-	G	-	B	-	D
Fm7	=	F	-	Ab	-	C	-	Eb
F#m7	=	F#	-	A	-	C#	-	E
Gbm7	=	Gb	-	Bbb	-	Db	-	Fb
Gm7	=	G	-	Bb	-	D	-	F
G#m7	=	G#	-	B	-	D#	-	F#

SEVENTH CHORDS WITH DIMINISHED FIFTH

Ab7-5	=	Ab	-	C	-	Ebb	-	Gb
A7-5	=	A	-	C#	-	Eb	-	G
A#7-5	=	A#	-	Cx	-	E	-	G#
Bb7-5	=	Bb	-	D	-	Fb	-	Ab
B7-5	=	B	-	D#	-	F	-	A
Cb7-5	=	Cb	-	Eb	-	Gbb	-	Bbb
C7-5	=	C	-	E	-	Gb	-	Bb
C#7-5	=	C#	-	E#	-	G	-	B
Db7-5	=	Db	-	F	-	Abb	-	Cb
D7-5	=	D	-	F#	-	Ab	-	C
D#7-5	=	D#	-	Fx	-	A	-	C#
Eb7-5	=	Eb	-	G	-	Bbb	-	Db
E7-5	=	E	-	G#	-	Bb	-	D
F7-5	=	F	-	A	-	Cb	-	Eb
F#7-5	=	F#	-	A#	-	C	-	E
Gb7-5	=	Gb	-	Bb	-	Dbb	-	Fb
G7-5	=	G	-	B	-	Db	-	F
G#7-5	=	G#	-	B#	-	D	-	F#

MINOR SEVENTH CHORDS WITH DIMINISHED FIFTH

Abm7-5	=	Ab	-	Cb	-	Ebb	-	Gb
Am7-5	=	A	-	C	-	Eb	-	G
A#m7-5	=	A#	-	C#	-	E	-	G#
Bbm7-5	=	Bb	-	Db	-	Fb	-	Ab
Bm7-5	=	B	-	D	-	F	-	A
Cbm7-5	=	Cb	-	Ebb	-	Gbb	-	Bbb
Cm7-5	=	C	-	Eb	-	Gb	-	Bb
C#m7-5	=	C#	-	E	-	G	-	B
Dbm7-5	=	Db	-	Fb	-	Abb	-	Cb
Dm7-5	=	D	-	F	-	Ab	-	C
D#m7-5	=	D#	-	F#	-	A	-	C#
Ebm7-5	=	Eb	-	Gb	-	Bbb	-	Db
Em7-5	=	E	-	G	-	Bb	-	D
Fm7-5	=	F	-	Ab	-	Cb	-	Eb
F#m7-5	=	F#	-	A	-	C	-	E
Gbm7-5	=	Gb	-	Bbb	-	Dbb	-	Fb
Gm7-5	=	G	-	Bb	-	Db	-	F
G#m7-5	=	G#	-	B	-	D	-	F#

SIXTH CHORDS

Ab6	=	Ab	-	C	-	Eb	-	F
A6	=	A	-	C#	-	E	-	F#
A#6	=	A#	-	Cx	-	E#	-	Fx
Bb6	=	Bb	-	D	-	F	-	G
B6	=	B	-	D#	-	F#	-	G#
Cb6	=	Cb	-	Eb	-	Gb	-	Ab
C6	=	C	-	E	-	G	-	A
C#6	=	C#	-	E#	-	G#	-	A#
Db6	=	Db	-	F	-	Ab	-	Bb
D6	=	D	-	F#	-	A	-	B
D#6	=	D#	-	Fx	-	A#	-	B#
Eb6	=	Eb	-	G	-	Bb	-	C
E6	=	E	-	G#	-	B	-	C#
F6	=	F	-	A	-	C	-	D
F#6	=	F#	-	A#	-	C#	-	D#
Gb6	=	Gb	-	Bb	-	Db	-	Eb
G6	=	G	-	B	-	D	-	E
G#6	=	G#	-	B#	-	D#	-	E#

MINOR SIXTH CHORDS

Abm6	=	Ab	-	Cb	-	Eb	-	F
Am6	=	A	-	C	-	E	-	F#
A#m6	=	A#	-	C#	-	E#	-	Fx
Bbm6	=	Bb	-	Db	-	F	-	G
Bm6	=	B	-	D	-	F#	-	G#
Cbm6	=	Cb	-	Ebb	-	Gb	-	Ab
Cm6	=	C	-	Eb	-	G	-	A
C#m6	=	C#	-	E	-	G#	-	A#
Dbm6	=	Db	-	Fb	-	Ab	-	Bb
Dm6	=	D	-	F	-	A	-	B
D#m6	=	D#	-	F#	-	A#	-	B#
Ebm6	=	Eb	-	Gb	-	Bb	-	C
Em6	=	E	-	G	-	B	-	C#
Fm6	=	F	-	Ab	-	C	-	D
F#m6	=	F#	-	A	-	C#	-	D#
Gbm6	=	Gb	-	Bbb	-	Db	-	Eb
Gm6	=	G	-	Bb	-	D	-	E
G#m6	=	G#	-	B	-	D#	-	E#

AUGMENTED CHORDS

Ab+	=	Ab	-	C	-	E
A+	=	A	-	C#	-	E#
A#+	=	A#	-	Cx	-	Ex
Bb+	=	Bb	-	D	-	F#
B+	=	B	-	D#	-	Fx
Cb+	=	Cb	-	Eb	-	G
C+	=	C	-	E	-	G#
C#+	=	C#	-	E#	-	Gx
Db+	=	Db	-	F	-	A
D+	=	D	-	F#	-	A#
D#+	=	D#	-	Fx	-	Ax
Eb+	=	Eb	-	G	-	B
E+	=	E	-	G#	-	B#
F+	=	F	-	A	-	C#
F#+	=	F#	-	A#	-	Cx
Gb+	=	Gb	-	Bb	-	D
G+	=	G	-	B	-	D#
G#+	=	G#	-	B#	-	Dx

AUGMENTED SEVENTH CHORDS

Ab7+	=	Ab	-	C	-	E	-	Gb
A7+	=	A	-	C#	-	E#	-	G
A#7+	=	A#	-	Cx	-	Ex	-	G#
Bb7+	=	Bb	-	D	-	F#	-	Ab
B7+	=	B	-	D#	-	Fx	-	A
Cb7+	=	Cb	-	Eb	-	G	-	Bbb
C7+	=	C	-	E	-	G#	-	Bb
C#7+	=	C#	-	E#	-	Gx	-	B
Db7+	=	Db	-	F	-	A	-	Cb
D7+	=	D	-	F#	-	A#	-	C
D#7+	=	D#	-	Fx	-	Ax	-	C#
Eb7+	=	Eb	-	G	-	B	-	Db
E7+	=	E	-	G#	-	B#	-	D
F7+	=	F	-	A	-	C#	-	Eb
F#7+	=	F#	-	A#	-	Cx	-	E
Gb7+	=	Gb	-	Bb	-	D	-	Fb
G7+	=	G	-	B	-	D#	-	F
G#7+	=	G#	-	B#	-	Dx	-	F#

DIMINISHED CHORDS

Abdim	=	Ab	-	Cb	-	Ebb
Adim	=	A	-	C	-	Eb
A#dim	=	A#	-	C#	-	E
Bbdim	=	Bb	-	Db	-	Fb
Bdim	=	B	-	D	-	F
Cbdim	=	Cb	-	Ebb	-	Gbb
Cdim	=	C	-	Eb	-	Gb
C#dim	=	C#	-	E	-	G
Dbdim	=	Db	-	Fb	-	Abb
Ddim	=	D	-	F	-	Ab
Ddim	=	D#	-	F#	-	A
Ebdim	=	Eb	-	Gb	-	Bbb
Edim	=	E	-	G	-	Bb
Fdim	=	F	-	Ab	-	Cb
F#dim	=	F#	-	A	-	C
Gbdim	=	Gb	-	Bbb	-	Dbb
Gdim	=	G	-	Bb	-	Db
G#dim	=	G#	-	B	-	D

DIMINISHED SEVENTH CHORDS

Abdim7	=	Ab	-	Cb	-	Ebb	-	Gbb (F)
Adim7	=	A	-	C	-	Eb	-	Gb
A#dim7	=	A#	-	C#	-	E	-	G
Bbdim7	=	Bb	-	Db	-	Fb	-	Abb (G)
Bdim7	=	B	-	D	-	F	-	Ab
Cbdim7	=	Cb	-	Ebb	-	Gbb	-	Bbbb (Ab)
Cdim7	=	C	-	Eb	-	Gb	-	Bbb (A)
C#dim7	=	C#	-	E	-	G	-	Bb
Dbdim7	=	Db	-	Fb	-	Abb	-	Cbb (Bb)
Ddim7	=	D	-	F	-	Ab	-	Cb (B)
D#dim7	=	D#	-	F#	-	A	-	C
Ebdim7	=	Eb	-	Gb	-	Bbb	-	Dbb (C)
Edim7	=	E	-	G	-	Bb	-	Db
Fdim7	=	F	-	Ab	-	Cb	-	Ebb (D)
F#dim7	=	F#	-	A	-	C	-	Eb
Gbdim7	=	Gb	-	Bbb	-	Dbb	-	Fbb (Eb)
Gdim7	=	G	-	Bb	-	Db	-	Fb (E)
G#dim7	=	G#	-	B	-	D	-	F

MAJOR SEVENTH CHORDS

AbM7	=	Ab	-	C	-	Eb	-	G
AM7	=	A	-	C#	-	E	-	G#
A#M7	=	A#	-	Cx	-	E#	-	Gx
BbM7	=	Bb	-	D	-	F	-	A
BM7	=	B	-	D#	-	F#	-	A#
CbM7	=	Cb	-	Eb	-	Gb	-	Bb
CM7	=	C	-	E	-	G	-	B
C#M7	=	C#	-	E#	-	G#	-	B#
DbM7	=	Db	-	F	-	Ab	-	C
DM7	=	D	-	F#	-	A	-	C#
D#M7	=	D#	-	Fx	-	A#	-	Cx
EbM7	=	Eb	-	G	-	Bb	-	D
EM7	=	E	-	G#	-	B	-	D#
FM7	=	F	-	A	-	C	-	E
F#M7	=	F#	-	A#	-	C#	-	E#
GbM7	=	Gb	-	Bb	-	Db	-	F
GM7	=	G	-	B	-	D	-	F#
G#M7	=	G#	-	B#	-	D#	-	Fx

MAJOR SEVENTH CHORDS WITH A MINOR THIRD

AbM7-3	=	Ab	-	Cb	-	Eb	-	G
AM7-3	=	A	-	C	-	E	-	G#
A#M7-3	=	A#	-	C#	-	E#	-	Gx
BbM7-3	=	Bb	-	Db	-	F	-	A
BM7-3	=	B	-	D	-	F#	-	A#
CbM7-3	=	Cb	-	Ebb	-	Gb	-	Bb
CM7-3	=	C	-	Eb	-	G	-	B
C#M7-3	=	C#	-	E	-	G#	-	B#
DbM7-3	=	Db	-	Fb	-	Ab	-	C
DM7-3	=	D	-	F	-	A	-	C#
D#M7-3	=	D#	-	F#	-	A#	-	Cx
EbM7-3	=	Eb	-	Gb	-	Bb	-	D
EM7-3	=	E	-	G	-	B	-	D#
FM7-3	=	F	-	Ab	-	C	-	E
F#M7-3	=	F#	-	A	-	C#	-	E#
GbM7-3	=	Gb	-	Bbb	-	Db	-	F
GM7-3	=	G	-	Bb	-	D	-	F#
G#M7-3	=	G#	-	B	-	D#	-	Fx

MAJOR SEVENTH CHORDS with MINOR THIRD and AUGMENTED FIFTH

AbM7-3+5	=	Ab	-	Cb	-	E	-	G
AM7-3+5	=	A	-	C	-	E#	-	G#
A#M7-3+5	=	A#	-	C#	-	Ex	-	Gx
BbM7-3+5	=	Bb	-	Db	-	F#	-	A
BM7-3+5	=	B	-	D	-	Fx	-	A#
CbM7-3+5	=	Cb	-	Ebb	-	G	-	Bb
CM7-3+5	=	C	-	Eb	-	G#	-	B
C#M7-3+5	=	C#	-	E	-	Gx	-	B#
DbM7-3+5	=	Db	-	Fb	-	A	-	C
DM7-3+5	=	D	-	F	-	A#	-	C#
D#M7-3+5	=	D#	-	F#	-	Ax	-	Cx
EbM7-3+5	=	Eb	-	Gb	-	B	-	D
EM7-3+5	=	E	-	G	-	B#	-	D#
FM7-3+5	=	F	-	Ab	-	C#	-	E
F#M7-3+5	=	F#	-	A	-	Cx	-	E#
GbM7-3+5	=	Gb	-	Bbb	-	D	-	F
GM7-3+5	=	G	-	Bb	-	D#	-	F#
G#M7-3+5	=	G#	-	B	-	Dx	-	Fx

MAJOR SEVENTH CHORDS with MINOR THIRD and DIMINISHED FIFTH

AbM7-3°5	=	Ab	-	Cb	-	Ebb	-	G
AM7-3°5	=	A	-	C	-	Eb	-	G#
A#M7-3°5	=	A#	-	C#	-	E	-	Gx
BbM7-3°5	=	Bb	-	Db	-	Fb	-	A
BM7-3°5	=	B	-	D	-	F	-	A#
CbM7-3°5	=	Cb	-	Ebb	-	Gbb	-	Bb
CM7-3°5	=	C	-	Eb	-	Gb	-	B
C#M7-3°5	=	C#	-	E	-	G	-	B#
DbM7-3°5	=	Db	-	Fb	-	Abb	-	C
DM7-3°5	=	D	-	F	-	Ab	-	C#
D#M7-3°5	=	D#	-	F#	-	A	-	Cx
EbM7-3°5	=	Eb	-	Gb	-	Bbb	-	D
EM7-3°5	=	E	-	G	-	Bb	-	D#
FM7-3°5	=	F	-	Ab	-	Cb	-	E
F#M7-3°5	=	F#	-	A	-	C	-	E#
GbM7-3°5	=	Gb	-	Bbb	-	Dbb	-	F
GM7-3°5	=	G	-	Bb	-	Db	-	F#
G#M7-3°5	=	G#	-	B	-	D	-	Fx

MAJOR SEVENTH CHORDS WITH A DIMINISHED FIFTH

AbM7°5	=	Ab	-	C	-	Ebb	-	G
AM7°5	=	A	-	C#	-	Eb	-	G#
A#M7°5	=	A#	-	Cx	-	E	-	Gx
BbM7°5	=	Bb	-	D	-	Fb	-	A
BM7°5	=	B	-	D#	-	F	-	A#
CbM7°5	=	Cb	-	Eb	-	Gbb	-	Bb
CM7°5	=	C	-	E	-	Gb	-	B
C#M7°5	=	C#	-	E#	-	G	-	B#
DbM7°5	=	Db	-	F	-	Abb	-	C
DM7°5	=	D	-	F#	-	Ab	-	C#
D#M7°5	=	D#	-	Fx	-	A	-	Cx
EbM7°5	=	Eb	-	G	-	Bbb	-	D
EM7°5	=	E	-	G#	-	Bb	-	D#
FM7°5	=	F	-	A	-	Cb	-	E
F#M7°5	=	F#	-	A#	-	C	-	E#
GbM7°5	=	Gb	-	Bb	-	Dbb	-	F
GM7°5	=	G	-	B	-	Db	-	F#
G#M7°5	=	G#	-	B#	-	D	-	Fx

MAJOR SEVENTH CHORDS WITH AUGMENTED FIFTH

AbM7+5	=	Ab	-	C	-	E	-	G
AM7+5	=	A	-	C#	-	E#	-	G#
A#M7+5	=	A#	-	Cx	-	Ex	-	Gx
BbM7v	=	Bb	-	D	-	F#	-	A
BM7+5	=	B	-	D#	-	Fx	-	A#
CbM7+5	=	Cb	-	Eb	-	G	-	Bb
CM7+5	=	C	-	E	-	G#	-	B
C#M7+5	=	C#	-	E#	-	Gx	-	B#
DbM7+5	=	Db	-	F	-	A	-	C
DM7+5	=	D	-	F#	-	A#	-	C#
D#M7+5	=	D#	-	Fx	-	Ax	-	Cx
EbM7+5	=	Eb	-	G	-	B	-	D
EM7+5	=	E	-	G#	-	B#	-	D#
FM7+5	=	F	-	A	-	C#	-	E
F#M7+5	=	F#	-	A#	-	Cx	-	E#
GbM7+5	=	Gb	-	Bb	-	D	-	F
GM7+5	=	G	-	B	-	D#	-	F#
G#M7+5	=	G#	-	B#	-	Dx	-	Fx

NINTH CHORDS

Ab	=	Ab	-	C	-	Eb	-	Gb	-	Bb
A9	=	A	-	C#	-	E	-	G	-	B
A#9	=	A#	-	Cx	-	E#	-	G#	-	B#
Bb9	=	Bb	-	D	-	F	-	Ab	-	C
B9	=	B	-	D#	-	F#	-	A	-	C#
Cb9	=	Cb	-	Eb	-	Gb	-	Bbb	-	Db
C9	=	C	-	E	-	G	-	Bb	-	D
C#9	=	C#	-	E#	-	G#	-	B	-	D#
Db9	=	Db	-	F	-	Ab	-	Cb	-	Eb
D9	=	D	-	F#	-	A	-	C	-	E
D#9	=	D#	-	Fx	-	A#	-	C#	-	E#
Eb9	=	Eb	-	G	-	Bb	-	Db	-	F
E9	=	E	-	G#	-	B	-	D	-	F#
F9	=	F	-	A	-	C	-	Eb	-	G
F#9	=	F#	-	A#	-	C#	-	E	-	G#
Gb9	=	Gb	-	Bb	-	Db	-	Fb	-	Ab
G9	=	G	-	B	-	D	-	F	-	A
G#9	=	G#	-	B#	-	D#	-	F#	-	A#

ELEVENTH CHORDS

Ab11	=	Ab	-	C	-	Eb	-	Gb	-	Bb	-	Db
A11	=	A	-	C#	-	E	-	G	-	B	-	D
A#11	=	A#	-	Cx	-	E#	-	G#	-	B#	-	D#
Bb11	=	Bb	-	D	-	F	-	Ab	-	C	-	Eb
B11	=	B	-	D#	-	F#	-	A	-	C#	-	E
Cb11	=	Cb	-	Eb	-	Gb	-	Bbb	-	Db	-	Fb
C11	=	C	-	E	-	G	-	Bb	-	D	-	F
C#11	=	C#	-	E#	-	G#	-	B	-	D#	-	F#
Db11	=	Db	-	F	-	Ab	-	Cb	-	Eb	-	Gb
D11	=	D	-	F#	-	A	-	C	-	E	-	G
D#11	=	D#	-	Fx	-	A#	-	C#	-	E#	-	G#
Eb11	=	Eb	-	G	-	Bb	-	Db	-	F	-	Ab
E11	=	E	-	G#	-	B	-	D	-	F#	-	A
F11	=	F	-	A	-	C	-	Eb	-	G	-	Bb
F#11	=	F#	-	A#	-	C#	-	E	-	G#	-	B
Gb11	=	Gb	-	Bb	-	Db	-	Fb	-	Ab	-	Cb
G11	=	G	-	B	-	D	-	F	-	A	-	C
G#11	=	G#	-	B#	-	D#	-	F#	-	A#	-	C#

THIRTEENTH CHORDS

Ab13	=	Ab	-	C	-	Eb	-	Gb	-	Bb	-	Db	-	F
A13	=	A	-	C#	-	E	-	G	-	B	-	D	-	F#
A#13	=	A#	-	Cx	-	E#	-	G#	-	B#	-	D#	-	Fx
Bb13	=	Bb	-	D	-	F	-	Ab	-	C	-	Eb	-	G
B13	=	B	-	D#	-	F#	-	A	-	C#	-	E	-	G#
Cb13	=	Cb	-	Eb	-	Gb	-	Bbb	-	Db	-	Fb	-	Ab
C13	=	C	-	E	-	G	-	Bb	-	D	-	F	-	A
C#13	=	C#	-	E#	-	G#	-	B	-	D#	-	F#	-	A#
Db13	=	Db	-	F	-	Ab	-	Cb	-	Eb	-	Gb	-	Bb
D13	=	D	-	F#	-	A	-	C	-	E	-	G	-	B
D#13	=	D#	-	Fx	-	A#	-	C#	-	E#	-	G#	-	B#
Eb13	=	Eb	-	G	-	Bb	-	Db	-	F	-	Ab	-	C
E13	=	E	-	G#	-	B	-	D	-	F#	-	A	-	C#
F13	=	F	-	A	-	C	-	Eb	-	G	-	Bb	-	D
F#13	=	F#	-	A#	-	C#	-	E	-	G#	-	B	-	D#
Gb13	=	Gb	-	Bb	-	Db	-	Fb	-	Ab	-	Cb	-	D
G13	=	G	-	B	-	D	-	F	-	A	-	C	-	E
G#13	=	G#	-	B#	-	D#	-	F#	-	A#	-	C#	-	E#